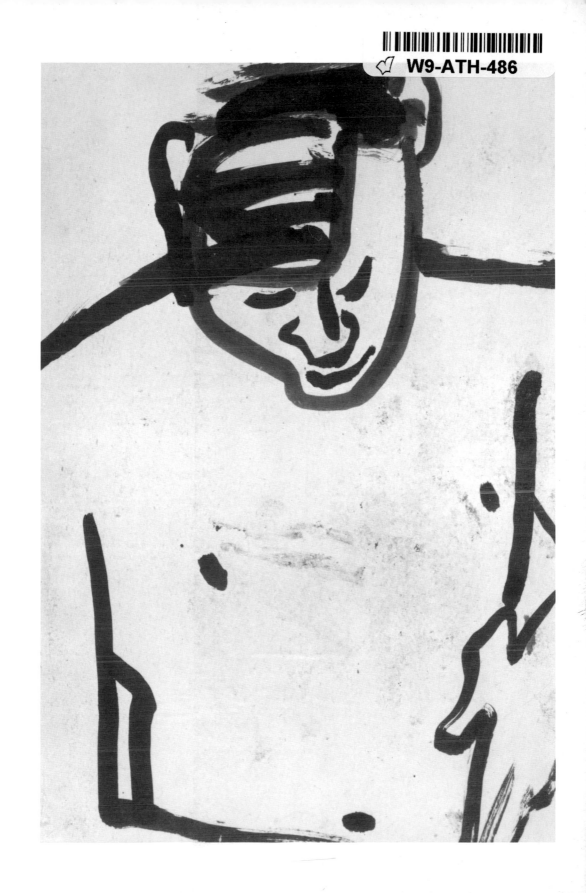

B. *David Park* by Richard
Diebenkorn, 1955,
pencil on paper.

C. *Self Portrait,* undated,
pencil on paper, 8 x 7.

THE NEW FIGURATIVE ART OF

David Park

by Paul Mills

CAPRA PRESS
Santa Barbara

To Jan;

to Lydia,
to Roy;

to Michael.

Their belief
and help
over many years
have made this book
possible.

Published by Capra Press
P.O. Box 2069
Santa Barbara
California 93120

Design/production by Margaret Dodd
of Yellow Dog Graphic Works
Text set in Leawood and Helvetica by
Tom Buhl Typographers
Printed by Chroma Litho
Photography of the Oakland Museum
paintings reproduced in color
by M. Lee Fatherree

Library of Congress Cataloging-in-
Publication Data
Mills, Paul Chadbourne, 1924-
The new figurative art of David Park
     p.   cm.
     Bibliography: p.
     ISBN 0-88496-295-4
     1. Park, David, 1911-1960 —
Criticism and interpretation.
I. Park, David, 1911-1960.
II. Oakland Museum. III. Title.
ND237.P24M54   1988   759.13 —
dc19
88-30247   CIP

CONTENTS

FOREWORD

T he important series of exhibitions of the paintings of David Park at the Whitney Museum of American Art in New York City, the Art Department of the Oakland Museum in Oakland, California, and elsewhere — not to mention the major exhibition of new figurative work sponsored by the San Francisco Museum of Modern Art in San Francisco, California — all, together, are giving me the push I needed, providing the opportunity to publish, at last, this major work on David Park.

This book is my most important research effort as an art historian and an art museum curator and director. I undertook it in 1961 and 1962, shortly after Park's death, in conjunction with my Master of Arts thesis at the University of California, Berkeley, and a Ford Foundation fellowship. It was the most extensive exploration undertaken by that time on a California-based modern painter.

It all began in the late fifties. I had been impressed with the work of the new figurative painters after being directed to it by Glenn Wessels and Fred Martin, and had organized their first group exhibition in 1959 while I was head of the Oakland Art Museum (now the Art Department of the Oakland Museum). Park, Richard Diebenkorn and Elmer Bischoff were central to that exhibition and indicated other artists they felt merited inclusion. I came to know all these artists fairly well.

I had initiated specialization in the art of California at the Oakland Art Museum, and when it came time for a topic for my M.A. thesis — which I was undertaking concurrently with my museum work — I spoke ardently, and successfully, for researching and writing on a California contemporary artist.

Quite naturally, I chose David Park, whose life had just come to an early and unexpected end in 1960, and who needed remembering and recording. I had found in preparing the text for the catalogue for the 1957 exhibition that artists, left to speak for themselves — with a little editing afterwards so they didn't sound too much like Gertrude Stein — were very eloquent about their art, about other artists and about issues of art. I expanded on that idea in my thesis research and had extensive interviews with those who had been close to Park, while his memory was still fresh and poignant in their minds. These people included Lydia, his wife, who was always most cooperative and candid; artists who were close to Park, including Diebenkorn and Bischoff, but many others as well; and members of his immediate family who knew him in his youth and through his development. I like the way they speak, and one of my roles has been to make it possible for the people who knew David best to tell their stories.

I have attempted to unclutter the book by having fewer footnotes than usually characterize a thesis. All quotations not specifically given a source are from conversations where I was present that took place roughly in the 1961 62 period. All material derived from written sources has been footnoted. Notations about specific paintings which exemplify a point just made are also footnoted. *General readers, not likely to be interested in such references, can cheerfully ignore all footnotes indicated by a number. The few I would like to ask them to read are indicated by an asterisk.*

This book has emerged and submerged repeatedly since it was written. It is hard to sort out all the people I would like to thank. Certainly among them is Lydia Park, now Mrs. Roy Moore, who has been consistently caring in every way. Roy Moore has cheerfully adopted David into his own family, and is very knowing about David's work and very generous about helping. My wife, Jan, made it possible for me to cope with both museum and master's degree back then, and has been just as encouraging and supportive in making this publication possible now. Without her, both David's posthumous life and my scholarship would have fared much less well. Everyone I talked to about David during my research was candid and honest, and I want to thank them — without them, there would be no book. In recent months, our son, Michael, an art student at Cooper Union in New York City, has been the ardent partisan of this book, whose constant, cheerful pressure has had much to do with my giving its publication the effort and time needed. The Salander-O'Reilly Galleries helped make it possible. Margaret Dodd, of Yellow Dog Graphic Works, has seen the design and production through splendidly, and I am most appreciative of the kind of attention to detail and friendly support she has given me. Noel Young has made it a special honor to be published by Capra Press of Santa Barbara, and has kept the publishing process a civilized and pleasant one, for which I thank him.

A special addition to the book is the color section reproducing all the David Park works in the collection of the Oakland Museum. Harvey Young, acting chief curator of the art department, and his staff, made that possible; my special thanks to them. Some of this collection goes back to my day; some of it is new. It is described in a note from Harvey preceding the reproductions on page 8.

Another publication of special interest to those who respond to Park, and which centers on artist interviews to an even greater extent than this book does, is Mary Fuller McChesney's *A Period of Exploration: San Francisco 1945-1950,* published by the Oakland Museum Art Department in 1973 in conjunction with an exhibition on the work of that era. I apparently only flipped through it when it came out; I have now come upon it again and read it carefully. I regard it as a remarkable document on its period which should be kept in print and become widely known.

Paul Chadbourne Mills
Santa Barbara, California
October 1988

Measurements are in inches;
height precedes width.

THE PARK PAINTINGS IN THE COLLECTION
OF THE ART DEPARTMENT, THE OAKLAND MUSEUM

The color reproductions present the paintings by David Park owned by the Art Department of the Oakland Museum. There are two groups, one acquired between 1959 and 1962, the other later. The museum staff was proud of having presented the first new figurative group exhibition in 1957 and became increasingly convinced of the importance of these artists; it therefore devoted most of the art acquisition funds during several years for purchase of their work. Three groups within the volunteer organization, the Oakland Museum Association — namely, the Art Guild, the Women's Board and an *ad hoc* Museum Donors Group — provided much of the funding; the rest came from an acquisition fund granted by an anonymous donor through the American Federation of Arts. The funds involved seem surprisingly modest in comparison with the value of the works today. Park works were chosen to show his development, including a little pre-abstract work, *Encounter (no. 3)*; the only remaining abstract expressionist work, *Non-Objective (Still Life — Non-Objective) (no. 4)*; the first new figurative work to be exhibited, *Rehearsal (no. 5)*; one of the most appealing works from the middle fifties, *Solitaire (no. 2)*; one of the grandest of all the late figurative paintings, *Women in a Landscape (no. 5)*; and a late work on paper, *Standing Nude Couple (no. 12, back cover)*.

Some years later, in 1965, Lydia Park (now Mrs. Roy Moore) lent a group of paintings to the museum, and in 1985 very generously gave many of them to the collection. These are fine works of Park's early and middle figurative manner, including *Early Portrait of Richard Diebenkorn (no. 7)*, *Audience (no. 6)*, *Tournament (no. 1, front cover)*, *Newspaper (no. 9)*, *Dancers (no. 8)* and *Boy in Striped Shirt (no. 10)*. She also gave many other early works on paper.

The museum thus has works of high quality marking the range of Park's art through the most important years of his development. It has, as well, fine paintings by Diebenkorn, Bischoff and other figurative artists.

Harvey Young
Acting Chief Curator of Art
The Oakland Museum

2. *Solitaire,* 1954?, oil on
canvas, 30 x 24¹/₄.
Purchased by the Art
Guild of the Oakland
Museum Association, 1962.

3. *Encounter,* 1945,
oil on masonite,
9 1/2 x 11 7/8. Purchased
by the Women's Board
of the Oakland Museum
Association, 1962.

4. *Non-Objective,* 1949,
oil on canvas, 34 x 25.
Purchased by the Women's
Board of the Oakland
Museum Association, 1962.

5. *Rehearsal,* 1949-50?, oil on
canvas, 46 x 35³/₄. Gift of an
anonymous donor through
the American Federation of
Arts, 1962.

6. *Audience,* 1953-54, oil on
canvas, 20 x 16. Gift of Mrs.
Roy Moore, 1985.

7. *Early Portrait of R.D. (Richard Diebenkorn),* 1954-55, oil on canvas, 20 x 14. Gift of Mrs. Roy Moore, 1985.

8. *Dancers,* undated,
oil on canvas, 16 x 24.
Gift of Mrs. Roy
Moore, 1985.

9. *Newspaper,* undated,
oil on canvas, 14 x 18.
Gift of Mrs. Roy
Moore, 1985.

10. *(right) Boy in Striped Shirt,*
1953?, oil on canvas, 25$^{7}/_{8}$ x 16.
Gift of Mrs. Roy Moore, 1985.

11. *Women in a Landscape,*
1958, oil on canvas, 50 x 56.
Gift of an anonymous donor
through the American
Federation of Arts, 1960.

INTRODUCTION

*I*n the bay area at the beginning of the fifties, while the momentum of post-war abstract expressionism was still increasing, certain paintings began to appear which indicated that one of the leading abstractionists, David Park, was propelling himself away from the abstract orbit into some new kind of course. His new work clearly and boldly reasserted a figurative, representational style. At first, this was regarded as only a personal heresy, but within a few years other notable artists were sharing this direction. Within the decade, this style became an embattled symbol of revolt against abstract expressionism; in truth, perhaps it was more a revolt against the limitations of avant gardism itself as a whole.

"The heroic age of American abstraction" is the title sometimes given to the decade or so following World War II, during which New York-based painters like de Kooning and Pollock, by remarkable acts of will and daring, brought American abstract expressionism into being. Their powerful "will to art," as critic John Coplans called it, created a painting style of stature and potency, high seriousness and uncompromising directness, which asserted the ability of American artists to challenge as never before the pre-eminence of Paris and Europe in modern art.

Yet abstract expressionism's unquestioned supremacy within the avant garde, even with the very painters who created it, was brief — hardly more than five years. Even while the movement was just beginning to gain recognition, defections occurred. Both de Kooning and Pollock returned, at least partially, to the figure within a few years. "Is our revolution imperiled so soon?", the spokesmen of abstract expressionism cried. Simultaneously in California, Park, then others, became early apostates.

This is the story of David Park. Its central concern is Park's new figurative style from its beginning in about 1950 to his death in 1960. His reintroduction of the

D. *David Park* by Richard
Diebenkorn, undated,
ink on paper.

Part One

THE CHANGE

THE SETTING

David Park was always a part of the life of the school before and during World War II. He did not start the explosion of energy which took place there after that war, but he was an important part of it — for a while. The development of abstract expressionism in the bay area and Park's change from it occurred primarily in the setting of the California School of Fine Arts and its parent organization, the San Francisco Art Association.* In the years after World War II, when most colleges experienced a sudden expansion brought on by returning veterans and government subsidies in the form of G.I. Bill funds, the California School of Fine Arts underwent an especially animated development. The veterans were mature, financially independent, frequently ready for advanced work, and possessed of certain emotional energies from their wartime service. They were quite unlike the usual college student body of high school graduates whose support came from their parents.

      Douglas MacAgy became director of the California School of Fine Arts in 1945. He designed his bold new administration around the opportunities the veterans made possible and catapulted the school into the front ranks of

---

* For clarity, the names used in Park's day, "San Francisco Art Association" and "California School of Fine Arts," will be used here, though it should be understood both of these are now known by the single name "San Francisco Art Institute." The association was subdivided into a patrons' membership and an artists' membership. When the association is referred to in this book, it is the artists' membership, whose principal public activity was sponsoring annual competitive exhibitions, which is meant.

contemporary art. A Canadian, thirty-two years old, he had studied at the University of Toronto, the Courtauld Institute, the University of Pennsylvania, the Barnes Foundation and Western Reserve University, served on the staff of the Wildenstein Gallery and was curator of the San Francisco Museum of Art from 1941 to 1943. His wife, Jermayne, became assistant director of the California Palace of the Legion of Honor museum in San Francisco and presented notably adventurous exhibitions in many fields.

MacAgy organized the school as an aggressive battalion of artists and novitiates pushing toward the front lines of modern art. Some of the more conservative members of the faculty were abruptly retired. Younger, more progressive members of the faculty — like Park, Hassel Smith and Elmer Bischoff, who had been on the periphery of the school, generally teaching only part-time — were brought into full-time positions. Though they were never the core of the MacAgy phalanx, they were swept up in what occurred, participated fully in it and were deeply altered by it.

The catalyst of the MacAgy era at the school was Clyfford Still, who soon had a national reputation as a leader of abstract expressionism. Still grew up in Spokane and Pullman, Washington, where he studied, taught art history and painted between the late twenties and World War II. He came to San Francisco in 1941 to work in war industry and had a virtually unnoticed one-man exhibition at the San Francisco Museum of Art. He was thereafter in the East for several years and in 1946 got significant recognition during a short stay in New York, exhibiting in Peggy Guggenheim's Arts of This Century Gallery with vanguard artists like Jackson Pollock, Mark Rothko, William Baziotes and Matta. He was soon familiar with all that had the ring of the avant garde about it in New York at the time. When MacAgy brought him to the school, Still came as a prophet of abstract expressionism and grew into the role with increasing relish. (He was not the first non-objective painter in the school; Charles Howard and perhaps others had a clearly defined — if not nearly so daring — non-objective style long before.) The first major presentation of Still's new work was a one-man show at the Palace of the Legion of Honor in 1948; it was generally regarded as the most significant solo avant garde exhibition of the era.

Still's work was committed to total abstraction; he claimed his work might possibly have some relation to past works of art, but it had none whatsoever to anything beyond paint on canvas and the artist's personality. Still and his followers made this absence of outside reference a very partisan issue and tried to force others in the school to "choose sides" over it. Any compromise with figuration was scorned. According to Fred Martin, artist and faculty member, then a student,

> "In their eyes, the forces of reaction had been identified."

Still's simple, craggy forms were organic in character, suggestive of — if anything — the forms of biology or geology. His chosen enemy was, as the critic Hubert Crehan said, "the impasse bequeathed by cubism" and its angular, architectural analysis of subject. Crehan, also a student in those days, wrote that Still's work

> "overlept [sic] the Cubist impasse entirely; it was not just a work in
> progress, experimental, but a fully mature new expression. Thereafter,

*for many artists in San Francisco the sense of discovery and investigation
of the possibilities of free-form painting was quickened; any fears that
there was no way out of the dilemma — that simple geometric
abstraction or representational Expressionism were the only alternatives
to Cubism — were exploded.''*[1]

Still also seemed to have a tough, direct paint quality, a boldness which
was admirable. Still's typical work today seems coldly controlled, even contrived, in
comparison with other abstract expressionists, but at the time his were among the
few, if not the only, surfaces of this sort which had been seen in California in any
number. Moreover, some of Still's earliest works actually *were* tougher and more
immediate. In *Untitled* (formerly *Self Portrait*) *(no. 20)*, painted about 1945, the black
background has a harsh, raw crudity about it; the principal linear form cutting
diagonally across it stumbles uncertainly and gracelessly, but somehow the whole
thing has a greater vitality, is more of an open, actual experience than the limited,
carefully edited schemes of his later paintings.

In the early days, when Park was more sympathetic to Still than he was
later, it was these more spontaneous paintings that he liked. Elmer Bischoff said,

*"I remember the reaction of David to Still's show at the Legion. David
singled out a couple of things that were not typical Stills at all. They were
cruder, I would say; they were rough kinds of things. He liked these, but
they were just one or two. . . . the things he liked of Still's were the much
more directly passionate things.''*

Park himself wrote,

*"Mondrian has pushed impersonal abstraction to the absolute limit;
Clyfford Still has pushed a free kind of emotional abstraction to another
limit.''*[2]

Richard Diebenkorn said Still's paintings

*"were immensely calculated, but it didn't seem so then. . . . they seemed
ragged and terribly immediate.''*

One of Still's most widely adopted innovations was the great size of his
paintings. Though his actual painting style was of less influence, the introduction of
big canvases provided a breakthrough for a number of incipient action painters
around the school. There had been an interest in free, spontaneous, energetic
abstraction, in linear calligraphic gesture. However, this had been held in by being
done on small canvases. Still's big sizes were picked up as the proper arena for
action painting even though Still himself was soon using these spaces in a very
different way. Hassel Smith said,

*"Most of the people here then would have said to themselves that Clyff was
the major influence [in encouraging action painting]. Now, looking back
on it, his work affected these people in a rather different way, because
there was little of what they were doing in his own work . . . Clyff's
influence on a lot of his associates' work resulted in a kind of appearance
that is totally different than his own painting. . . The reason for this is fairly*

concrete; the size of his canvases was a major factor. None of us had seen anything approaching that dimension. The idea of overcoming the limitations that smaller canvases had on activity, particularly among young and inexperienced painters, created a kind of muscularity which came out of a need to do something in such a large area. . . . I don't think they ever really understood the character of his own work."

Still also set an example in his personal relation to his art. He was totally committed, uncompromising, brutal and intense in his integrity. He insisted that his work be regarded with awe, as though, perhaps, it were radioactive, and once said — his most quoted remark —

"A painting in the wrong hands is a highly dangerous force, just like a mathematical equation. . . Let no man undervalue the implications of his work or its power for life, or for death, if it is misused."[3]

While only a few chose to emulate this aspect of Still — and, as we shall see, Park and others came to abhor it — the presence of such coldly burning dedication in the midst of a group of artists had its effect.

In addition to Still, there was, at least briefly, another Eastern vanguard artist of considerable note at the school. This was Mark Rothko, who, probably at the suggestion of Still, came to teach in the summer sessions of 1947 and 1949. His work was in a formative stage and less well known. He was at first doing surrealist calligraphies against amorphous washes, and only later began the distinctive planes of burning color for which he is well known.

The students and faculty at the school responded in one way or another to this powerful impact. Painters like Edward Dugmore and Ernest Briggs remained closest to Still's teachings. Others, like John Grillo (who arrived in 1945 before Still), Edward Corbett, Lawrence Calcagno, John Hultberg and Richard Diebenkorn, made strong "post cubist" statements affected by Still or Rothko.

Many advanced students and progressive young artists in the association worked quite independently of the official example of MacAgy, Still and Rothko. In some cases, according to Alfred Frankenstein, veteran critic and art historian,

". . . it was the students who pushed the faculty toward new experimental work."

These young artists were quick to go off on their own parallel but independent paths and to paint, exhibit and exchange ideas in aggressive separation from the school. They developed a number of personal abstract idioms and manners for which there was no direct example in the work of the faculty. Many centered their activities around the Metart and King Ubu galleries.

Hassel Smith, Elmer Bischoff and David Park also plunged deeply into the abstract tide. They did not deny cubism so totally as Still, but they were more spontaneous, more varied. In place of the rigid domination of a single rationale which Still imposed on his imagery, they presented confusing variation, rawness and recklessness. They exhibited together at the San Francisco Museum of Art in 1949 in a show which had even more of an impact on the bay area public than the Still show of the year before. Erle Loran, painter and University of

California art department faculty member, described the reaction in his San Francisco column for *Art News:*

> *"It was the most complete release from restraints of all kinds that had ever occurred. Even the overloaded blacks, browns and whites of Clyfford Still [exhibited previously at the Legion of Honor] seemed composed and orderly by comparison with many paintings of this group. . . . The work of Bischoff and Park is notable for its strong emphasis on paint—what the French call* matière. *Most of the painters of this new trend take unprecedented delight in the handling, smearing, splotching, piling up of the pigment surface. The ferocious attack evident in the pigment application of Jackson Pollack's [sic] work comes to mind too, and if no other positive plastic value existed, this emphasis on the surface itself would be well worth consideration, even emulation. It is a new, almost unconscious biological reaffirmation of the primacy of the two-dimensional picture plane in painting. Before any separate shapes emerge one assumes that the whole pictorial surface has been brought to life spontaneously, as an entity, with richly loaded colors and textures. Some forms and color shapes finally do emerge but seldom with finality and completeness."*[4]

Part of the impact of the show was the size of the paintings; they outdid Still's work on that score too. Fred Martin remembered Park's work in this show as being

> *"the biggest paintings I had ever seen. . . . They were the size of the whole wall, it seemed."*

Diebenkorn remembers the show as being

> *"expressionistic and pretty wild. They were interested in jazz at the time and in a kind of free wheeling, wide-open, totally generous kind of thing. People were seriously shocked. They had been a bit more in awe of the Still show."*

This show was, for Park at least, his farthest reach into abstract expressionism. It was, though, quite a different facet of abstract expressionism than that which Still developed. As the Loran review points out, Park's work was notable for its exuberant spontaneity and its extreme use of paint, which went far beyond anything Still had done. Yet, it was essentially less abstract than Still's work; where Still stood for a total denial of any reference whatsoever, Park never went as far. Often paintings which seemed totally devoid of any reference were really covertly figurative. Martin remembers that, in the late forties, he and Sam Francis rented a Park painting from the San Francisco Museum rental service—a companion piece to *Non-Objective (no. 21)*—thinking it totally devoid of reference, only to realize some time later that it was a vase of flowers. Martin said,

> *"It turned out later, if you knew it, they probably all were based on some kind of hidden representation."*

Diebenkorn remembered a similar incident.

"It was at the high point of abstract expressionism. I would say it was 1949. One day in his little studio at the school he was working on a painting. The lower half was a big whitish shape, with a couple of purple spots on it. We were considering it together, and it came out in the discussion that those spots were the shadows of birds and that the white was a wall. This was at the height of the abstract expressionist thing, and it was very surprising to me that he would do this."

Speaking of the reappearance of recognizable figuration in Park's work, Martin said,

"I always saw his paintings in a representational way. The change was no shock to me. . . All he did then was just let the figurative source show a little more."

Even on the matter of the expressionist nature of this kind of painting Still and Park differed. Where Still was, as Diebenkorn saw it,

". . . intellectually and conceptually developed totally as an abstract expressionist, for David it was a kind of temporary release, which is the reason it was such a brief thing. He never believed in it; there was something he wasn't 'supposed' to do — there was something 'bad' — about it; he was really 'smearing it on' and being irresponsible about it."

By 1950, the post-war surge at the school showed clear signs of beginning to dissipate. The ranks of the veterans began to thin, enrollment at the school declined, important figures like Still and Rothko had left or were on the verge of leaving, young high school graduates reappeared on the horizon. Though abstraction remained the dominant mode, the initial tide of organized support for it began to ebb and subside into scattered pools and eddies. The partially submerged individualities of artists like Park and Bischoff came to the surface again and they reasserted an independent, though altered, position.

David Park was one of the first artists to take a personal stance and certainly the first to take a new direction. In March 1950, at the San Francisco Art Association members' show at the De Young Museum, he exhibited a painting of a jazz band called *Rehearsal (nos. 5 & 22)*. It was simple, straightforward and archly innocent in its realism, yet elements in it had been shoved into strange, aggressive foreshortening. Something in the handling of the paint still had the manner of abstract expressionism. It was a portrait of the jazz band at the school in which he and other faculty members played. It perplexed and disturbed those who knew him but, in the variety of this unjuried members' show, it went unnoticed and caused no recorded comment.

The following year, in March 1951, the next of these perplexing figurative paintings of Park's, *Kids on Bikes (no. 24)*, was accepted for the San Francisco Art Association's annual exhibition, a much more competitive and serious open exhibition than the members' show. It was obvious now that Park was making a deliberate, calculated move away from abstract expressionism. However, it was quite unclear whether he was moving forward or backward; his use of representation was a return, but the style was strangely inconsistent with the canons of either abstract expressionism or earlier figurative art. The figure of a boy in a striped shirt on a bike became huge as it pushed into the foreground of the picture. A much tinier bicyclist in a brilliant white shirt rode away in the background. A fence slammed precipitously from the foreground back deep into the picture. In spite of these bold assertions of space, the flat color planes and surface texture prevented the picture from escaping two-dimensional flatness entirely. The deliberate innocence of the subject was entirely remarkable. The jury gave it a prize and it was reproduced in the catalogue, the local papers, the Art Association's bulletin and in the national magazine *Art Digest,* though the critics avoided any written comments about it.

Park was launched on an independent and uncertain course which led him beyond the bounds of any recognized style or movement.

1. Hubert Crehan, "Is There a California School?", *Art News,* January 1955, vol. 54, no. 9, pp. 32-35.
2. Alfred Frankenstein, "Northern California," *Art in America,* Winter 1954, vol. 42, no. 1, p. 49.
3. Quoted, *Time,* vol. 74, no. 19, November 9, 1959, pp. 80-83.
4. Erle Loran, "San Francisco," *Art News,* September 1949, vol. 48, no. 6, p. 45.

EARLY LIFE

*E*xperiences of Park's early life prepared him considerably to play the role he did in the fifties. A summary of it will help make his reasons for the change and his new cause more understandable. Born in Boston in 1911, the son of a Unitarian minister, he was brought up in a circle of well-educated people — verbal, even eloquent, literary, to some extent artistic. David was a rather awkward, earnest child, somehow always at the periphery of his family's life. His brother was active in sports but David was not; he preferred painting, playing the piano and creating puppet shows, and was a poor student. His immediate family was confused by his lack of its usual traits and interests, but an understanding aunt who was an art teacher, and several similar women, encouraged and counseled him. His aunt, Mrs. John F. Truesdell — his father's sister — gave him a certain special understanding both in his early years and in his late teens in California. She put it very precisely.

"David was the 'off chicken.' He was a slow blossomer. . . almost a black sheep. His brother Richard was active in sports. David was neither student nor sportsman. He liked painting, playing the piano, puppet shows; he wore glasses. He used to spend weekends with us. He would debate about his future: would he be a painter?. . . or a pianist? Usually he decided to be a painter."

Another mentor of his youth, Louisa R. Alger, wrote,

"I first met David when he was a sensitive, odd, charming boy of perhaps 13, and I was a new teacher, green as grass after my first year. David and I were visitors for a month or more of two sisters, the head of my school and the head of his. David took a liking to me and used to follow me around; he said, 'Why do you use such long words?' I remember debating the point and (knowing that his own family was highly literate and used just as long words as mine) arguing that my words were not long.

Looking back, I realize it was a critical time in his life. Frances Lee (my head) was a good painter in both watercolor and oils; her friend Mary Gay painted well enough to have exhibited her oils in the Paris Salon. Those two women and David made a delightful trio when they discussed their painting. Mary Gay watched over his work that summer and every now and then gave him a pointer. I remember the great satisfaction of the two elders when David was commissioned — for five dollars — to paint a neighbor's garden then in full blossom. And David's solemn and intense joy as he painted, as he completed the work, as it was approved by the patron, as he received the five dollars!"[5]

In high school, Park continued to fall short of the scholastic standards of his family. He did not make it to college. He is supposed to have said some years later that he deliberately failed examinations to avoid college; at least it is certain he was reluctant to go. Instead, he came to live with his aunt and uncle, then in Los Angeles, who arranged for him to attend Otis Art Institute there in 1928, with Vitlacil as his principal teacher.

In 1929, he moved to San Francisco to attend summer sessions at the University of California in Berkeley, but he was soon instead involved with the world of artists in San Francisco. He shared a place with another young art student, Gordon Newell, on Telegraph Hill. Newell is today one of the few California sculptors continuing to work in large stone pieces, and lives in Monterey. Park soon met and happily married Newell's sister, Lydia, in 1930.

David and Lydia Park lived in the bay area for six years, generally in Berkeley. These were the years of the depression, of the New Deal, and of the Federal Arts Project under the Works Progress Administration (W.P.A.). He worked on many projects. In San Francisco, Park and Gordon Newell both served as stonecutters and assistants to the sculptor Ralph Stackpole on his two monumental stone figures in front of the San Francisco stock exchange. Park also did a mural (DP1104), typical of the times, glorifying various forms of art, labor and industry for the John Muir School, carefully composed with considerable concern for the relation of contours. He designed a pair of tapestries (DP1101) for the library of Piedmont High School, depicting classical figures, perhaps muses, with the kind of attention to abstract shapes created by the fall of light which he was to explore more fully later. It is one of the handsomest of his early works. He also did a frieze-like mural (DP1518) for the music building at Mills College in Oakland — known now only through photographs — of Bacchic dancers with cymbals and flageolets. It was in a style and a medium — tempera on gesso, in this case on plywood — popular with other muralists of the time. Unfortunately, the donor did not like it and rejected it; later, it was cut up and turned into ping pong tables.*

His work in these days was not notably different from the typical painter's and muralist's work of the time. He painted the heavy, simplified groups of figures, exemplifying allegories or public themes, which the bay area learned from the Mexican muralists, particularly Diego Rivera, who had a strong influence. If he differed in any respect, he was less concerned about the wider social significance of his subject than the average painter, more concerned with the human figure and its interplay of shapes and contours.

In 1936 the Parks, who by now had two daughters — Natalie, born in 1931 (now Natalie Park Schutz) and Helen, born in 1933 (now Helen Park Bigelow) — moved to Boston. Park took a position teaching art on the faculty of Winsor School, a distinguished private school for girls near Boston. His aunt had established the art department and it was through her that Park made his original contact. During the five years he stayed, as the work remaining from that period indicates, Park started from figure paintings rather like Thomas Hart Benton's and became increasingly involved with a synthetic cubism which took certain aspects of Picasso's work of the mid twenties as its principal example. By the end of the thirties he was skillful in handling most of the cubist devices.

In 1941 the Parks, tired of the limitations of teaching in a girls' school, returned to California. World War II began shortly after. Throughout the war, Park

---

* In a letter dated September 15, 1988, Philip E. Linhares, Director of the Mills College Art Gallery, informed the author that the mural panels from the music building have been found. Gryffyd Partridge wrote on August 30, 1988, that in the fifties he was a project planner for the San Francisco Housing Authority, where leftover Federal Arts Project work had been stored. He noted the David Park panels, and called Park, who stated he had advanced to another phase of his work and was totally disinterested in them. They ended up in the Almonte Improvement Club in Mill Valley, and were used to make tables for meetings and other purposes. Now, some 33 years later, efforts are being made to reclaim them. Except for hinge holes, they are in surprisingly good condition. Almost all the figures are classical in togas holding musical instruments. There are a few figures in modern pants, and a few horses. There has been some speculation that these are "sketches" for murals, but they looked to Partridge like the actual murals themselves. There are a few moments when the depictions are a bit disappointing, but on the whole the figures, especially the classical ones, are handsomely and boldly depicted, in a manner generally like the Piedmont High School tapestries, and well merit being put in an appropriate architectural setting.

worked for the General Cable Company in Emeryville, generally on the night shift, in an atmosphere which he found refreshingly different and where he acquired an enthusiasm for salty limericks. Somehow he managed to paint at least a little every day, though his work from this period is relatively thin and unambitious. During these war years, he redeveloped his contact with the San Francisco Art Association and the California School of Fine Arts and taught classes at the San Francisco Museum of Art, as well as Art League of the East Bay children's classes at the Oakland Art Gallery.[6] He began teaching at the School of Fine Arts in 1944 and became a full-time faculty member shortly after.

Throughout his life, Park had found himself somewhat outside convention and had become mildly irreverent toward it. He was easily drawn to what was progressive in the arts, though he had always been content to participate in small avant garde movements in which others were the leaders. However, the nature of the abstract expressionist movement and the school itself caused him to go one step further, to reject it in exasperation and to change to an entirely personal and independent kind of painting.

5. Louisa R. Alger; letter to the author, February 6, 1962.
6. (later Oakland Art Museum, now Art Department, The Oakland Museum)

EXTERNAL INFLUENCES

Some of the reasons for Park's change were personal and internal, stemming from his character as an artist. Others had to do with external situations and his reaction to them. The main outer situations which made Park move toward figurative painting again were the cult which had developed around the personality of Clyfford Still — which he found distasteful — and the decline of the school after the G.I. Bill period.

Throughout most of his years at the school Park had the difficult role of being a loyal dissenter. He believed in the school and in the art association allied with it, but he fought stubbornly against certain policies.

Hassel Smith knew both Still and Park well at the school in the post-war forties. Although Smith had considerable admiration for Still, his work struck Smith as being "almost fussy; a very elegant and fussy kind of painting." Smith saw Still's art as an accurate expression of his personality, which was a decided contrast to Park's. Smith once said,

> *"The appearance of Still's studio was indicative of the manner in which he worked. There would be no signs of any work. There would be this little glass palette, perfectly cleaned off, a little, perfectly clean rag and a perfectly clean palette knife laid on the table next to it. You have to recognize in this painting a very compulsive neatness. A certain deep, personal, subjective tendency about such things as neatness or messiness is more influential than is generally recognized. It affects the character of the artist's work more pervasively than any question of talent or exterior influence. Clyff was the sort of guy who never permitted himself any messing around.*
>
> *In his personal appearance, he dressed more like a businessman. He wore a Homburg hat, a grey suit and tie and frequently he even wore grey gloves. He wore a muffler and an overcoat and perpetually seemed like he was chilly... Clyff is a guy totally devoid of a sense of humor and as the years have gone by he has lost what little humor he had and has become practically psychopathic in the sense of his own importance."*

According to Elmer Bischoff,

> *"Still was the big hero as far as MacAgy and a small group of students were concerned. He maintained a position of aloofness, as an outsider coming in. My feeling was he wasn't too keen about being connected with the faculty. When Rothko was here they would be together all the time, having coffee in the coffee shop or whatever, but he didn't have an immediate personal thing with the rest of the faculty — there was no great connectiveness. He had his sphere of influence, but it was behind closed doors with a particular group of students."*

Park was a very different sort of person. He was a kind of "debunker." He had a liking for what was unpretentious and pleasant in life. His sense of humor and of ridicule made it impossible for him to take anyone like Still very seriously. He approached most situations with sincerity but a kind of tentativeness; he was willing to try out all sorts of ideas, but quickly subjected anything inflated or vulnerable to ridicule.

Park, like everyone else at the school, was at first deeply affected by the concepts of abstraction for which Still was spokesman and responded especially to the "action painting" aspects. However, as Still's work became more of a stereotyped rational formula and as Still heightened his emphasis on its occult, quasi-religious significance, Park became increasingly disenchanted with it. According to Bischoff,

> *"I would say that David's reaction to Still as Still's work got more 'cosmological' was one of less and less sympathy. I surmise that his reaction to non-representational painting of Still's sort was that it had gotten too serious-minded, gotten into pretentiousness. David was keen*

> *about abstract expressionism as long as it had that immediacy and*
> *tangibility and goopy sensuous arrangement of forms, but when it got*
> *into very serious 'views of the cosmos' he didn't go along with that.*
> *As these paintings became less directly sensuous, more austere,*
> *more 'religious,' he felt that they really ran the risk of becoming just*
> *big decorations."*

Park's natural skepticism and sense of the ridiculous was incompatible with it. When he saw how easily such pretentious paintings could be treated simply as decorations and used as settings for fashion photographs or in smart interiors, he was further distressed. He told the author some years later,

> *"Art ought to be a troublesome thing, and one of my reasons for painting*
> *representationally is that this makes for much more troublesome*
> *pictures."*[7]

Before long, the circle of painters and students around Still came to have much of the character of an esoteric and questionable cult which Park gradually began to oppose. Hassel Smith said,

> *"The initial impact of Clyff's work was really very strong on everyone.*
> *Rather quickly, Dave began to feel a real antipathy toward it. He began to*
> *promote a kind of counter-influence among the students and his friends.*
> *Dave felt rather strongly that the Still influence was a pernicious one.*
> *Dave's approach was in part influenced by what he saw, and what he*
> *came to object to, in the effect that Still had on the students. He had a*
> *teacher's interest in part and the development of this sort of cult around*
> *Clyff, composed of a certain group of students, was a bad thing for the*
> *school, he felt, and he may have been perfectly right about that.*
> *I don't believe Clyff promoted that cult himself, but it happened. After a*
> *comparatively short time, Dave began to feel pretty strongly that non-*
> *objective painting of Still's sort was a dead end, and that it developed*
> *toward a pretentious and obscure kind of thing which he began to take a*
> *position against even while he was painting non-objectively himself and*
> *very enthusiastically."*

Park not only opposed the Still cult, which by no means ended with Still's departure, but gradually came into increasingly open and active opposition to the MacAgy regime on other scores. Park respected what MacAgy had accomplished at the school. However, MacAgy and his visiting luminaries like Still and Rothko tended to have all the advantages while local teachers were paid poorly and led an insecure existence. Park led the fight for broader rights and advantages for the faculty as a whole and took an active and effective part in school politics. When the G.I. Bill money began to run out and Still and MacAgy left, the school had to begin retrenching. The problems which concerned Park became worse instead of better. When money continued to decrease, cuts in staff were made, infighting and internal wrangling became worse, and some of the most progressive people were dropped. When Hassel Smith was dismissed, Park and Bischoff resigned. Bischoff said,

> *"We thought our leaving was a gesture that might cause a reaction — that it*
> *would put an end to it."*

The reaction did not occur; the school only moved further in a conservative direction. An era was over.*

E. *David Park* by Richard Diebenkorn, undated, pencil on paper.

* At this point, it is appropriate to read Park's own "Detailed Account of Career as Student and Creative Artist" (courtesy of Helen Park Bigelow), apparently written in 1952, printed in the 1987 Salander-O'Reilly Galleries catalogue, *David Park,* which has a number of especially interesting short articles, remains in print, and is well worth reading.

> *"My interest in painting began in early childhood. A landscape, painted when I was fourteen and exhibited in a no-jury show in Boston, was purchased by Mrs. Juliana Force for what was then the Whitney Studio Club.*
>
> *After completing the college preparatory course at the Loomis School in Windsor, Connecticut (1928), I entered the Otis Art Institute in Los Angeles, where after three weeks I was promoted to the advanced classes in painting.*
>
> *In 1929 I moved to San Francisco and worked for a year as stone-cutter for Ralph Stackpole who was executing a large sculpture commission for the San Francisco Stock Exchange. In 1930 I married and took a job in a blue-printing plant. During this period I was painting in my spare time.*

I first taught painting in 1931-32 at the Greenwood School, Berkeley (a private school for children). Thereafter until 1936 I taught painting classes at the Bentley School (another private school in Berkeley). During these years I also taught drawing and painting at the University of California Extension Division. Within this same period I completed several projects sponsored by the Federal Works of Art and W.P.A. Art Programs. These were: a series of watercolors of different W.P.A. labor projects; a group of three frescos in the entrance hall of the John Muir School in San Francisco; and later, a frieze, executed in tempera and made up of eleven panels, each four by twelve feet. These were subsequently installed at the San Francisco Golden Gate Exposition on Treasure Island.

In 1936 I was appointed head of the Art Department at the Winsor School in Boston. I had two assistants and the department offered painting and sculpture in various media, metal, wood and leather craft, and stage design for the school's numerous dramatic activities. Since the Winsor School was one of the "thirty schools" which, under the Progressive Education Association, were attempting to improve pre-college education, I had additional responsibilities as representative of the school at many conferences in New York and Boston. After five years in this position, in spite of considerable inducements (financial and other) to remain, I felt obliged to return to Berkeley on account of family responsibilities.

I resumed teaching at the University of California Extension Division (1941) where I also introduced a new course for secondary school teachers. At about this time I initiated classes for amateurs at the San Francisco Museum of Art.

In teaching I have deliberately tried to develop the student's reliance on inner, imaginative resources. Whereas most students, in my experience, approach painting with an alert sense of the claims of naturalistic representation, their responses to such qualities as expressiveness, sensitivity and formal vitality stand relatively in need of cultivation.

During the war I worked in a cable manufacturing plant as crane operator and later in charge of one of their processing departments. In 1944 I was asked to teach night school at the California School of Fine Arts and did this in addition to the industrial job.

At the close of the war, Douglas MacAgy, the newly appointed director of the California School of Fine Arts, asked me to teach a full program including both day and evening classes, and throughout his administration I enjoyed a most stimulating environment for both teaching and painting. In the summer sessions of 1948 I was asked to give two courses at the University of California Art Department in Berkeley.

In the summer of 1950, after Mr. MacAgy left the school, I had the responsibilities of Acting Director. But with the appointment, that fall, of the present director, it became clear to me that the school would be guided toward aims that I do not believe valid, and I finally left the school in February, 1952. I have since been working night shift in an industrial plant and painting.

I have served on the Artists' Council of the San Francisco Art Association from 1946-51, and as its chairman two of those years. I have recently compiled a book of reproductions of work of sixty-eight members of the association which is being published by the University of California Press under the title "Painting and Sculpture — The San Francisco Art Association." It will be off the press this month.

I have been elected to serve on Art Association juries four or five times and in 1946 I was appointed one of the judges for the Albert M. Bender Grants-in-Aide and similarly in 1951 one of the judges for the Rosenburg Travelling Fellowship.

The only juried exhibitions to which I have regularly submitted paintings have been the annuals of the San Francisco Art Association. My first entry, in 1931, was accepted and my work has been included quite regularly ever since. In their Annual of 1935 I received an award for "String Quartet" and again in 1950 for "Kids on Bikes." "The Red Jug" was accepted in 1946 for the California Palace of the Legion of Honor's first annual exhibition of contemporary American painting—(since changed to an invitational show). Also my "Shore Line" was accepted this summer at the California State Fair.

In 1936 "String Quartet" was invited to the Chicago Art Institute Annual. In 1952 "Sunbather" was invited to the University of Illinois Exhibition of Contemporary American Painting.

The San Francisco Museum of Art has for the past ten years annually presented exhibitions of Bay Region Artists which have regularly included my work. Many of those exhibitions have been sent out as travelling shows."

7. *Contemporary Bay Area Figurative Painting*, Oakland Art Museum, Oakland, California, 1957, p. 7.

INTERNAL REASONS

*B*eyond external situations like Still's influence and the decline of the school which encouraged Park to change from abstraction, internal, personal reasons, revealed in the remarks of other artists who knew him then and in his own statements, were stronger forces pushing for a change.

Park was seldom notably successful in his abstract efforts. His friends felt so and he seemed to feel so himself. James McCray, who knew him fairly well, said,

". . . he seemed to be a little on the defensive about his abstractions. . . . We were both on the board of the San Francisco Art Association together. When I went to the school for meetings, I would stop in to see David. He was always working — he had paintings spread all around him — he seemed to have four to five wet ones at a time. It wasn't working the way he wanted it to — he was always working with a wet, oily surface trying to push the stuff around here and there and trying to make it come off. I don't think he was really very satisfied with it."

Diebenkorn felt Park's abstract expressionism was

". . . kind of forced. . . he was involved with shape but I never felt there was a terribly important space to his non-objective work. . . . There would be shapes without a good reason, there would be shapes which were representational — they were awkward and got in the way. . . The abstract expressionist period was. . . the weakest period of all his work. He couldn't find the disciplines in this way of working. He needed some kind of counter in his work."

Bischoff said, though he felt

". . . the reaction against Still was not out of the question as a reason for his dissatisfaction, I would have to say it was basically a very personal thing. It was a matter of just playing these forms out. It was just getting stupid. The fact that he threw away most of his non-objective work speaks for itself. . . Park was not primarily motivated by a reaction to Still, he was only spirited on by it, he was given more fire by it."

He painted prolifically but his attitude toward the results is indicated by the fact that he took all the abstract paintings in his studio — with two exceptions, one of them *Non-Objective (nos. 4 & 21)* — and painted over them or took them to the Berkeley city dump and destroyed them.

Park's own statements are even better evidence that the reasons for his change were personal. His words not only express his dependence on inner processes but tell us to some extent what these processes were. He wrote the clearest, most basic statement of what he thought art to be and of how the artist could create it for the catalogue of the one-man exhibition at the De Young Museum in San Francisco in spring 1959.

"I think of painting — in fact all the arts — as a sort of extension of human life. The very same things that we value most, the ideals of humanity, are the properties of the arts. The words that come to mind are many — energy, wisdom, courage, delight, humor, sympathy, gentleness, honesty, peace, freedom — I believe most artists are goaded by a vision of making their work vivid and alive with such qualities. I believe this is the undercurrent of the artist's energy.

He cannot work with such self-consciousness as to be actually preoccupied by this undercurrent; instead he must work with a kind of total absorption that permits the undercurrent to operate automatically. His choice of subject, or his immediate painting objective is whatever invites him to paint with total absorption. He often prefers not to attempt to explain his work because on the one hand he needs to avoid self-consciousness and on the other, he knows that the immediate or surface aspect of his painting is only the means by which he can get in gear with those undercurrents that make art an extension of life."[8]

Park was not one to make manifestos on behalf of his new painting. However, he did make public statements about his reasons for the change several times in the early fifties. The first was written for the catalogue of the University of Illinois exhibition of contemporary American painting in 1952.

"I like to paint subjects that I know and care about: people, singly and in crowds, in commonly seen attitudes. I like to paint my friends. It is exciting to me to try to get some of the subject's qualities, whether warmth, vitality, harshness, tenderness, solemnness or gaiety into a picture. For instance, if I am painting a sunbather on a beach [his entry in the exhibition was Sunbather *(no. 37)] I want it to be warm and open and simple and solid and light-hearted, and yet heavy with relaxation, and it should also have the freshness of clean air. I believe that I was thinking about these and many such things when I painted that picture.*

I believe the best painting America has produced is in the current non-objective direction. However, I often miss the sting that I believe a more descriptive reference to some fixed subject can make. Quite often, even the very fine non-objective canvases seem to me to be so visually beautiful that I find them insufficiently troublesome, not personal enough."[9]

The other written statement of the reasons for his change is from 1953. It appears in two somewhat different versions, one in the little publication *Artist's View,* published briefly "by Painters, Poets and Sculptors" in San Francisco, which devoted an issue to photographs of his work and a statement by him in September 1953, the month after his first new figurative one-man show at the King Ubu Gallery in San Francisco.[10] The other version is in the article by Alfred Frankenstein on Northern California for *Art in America*'s first annual issue on "Americans with a Future," published in winter 1954.[11] The following combines what is unique in both versions.

"The reproductions on these pages are from work done in the past three years. I call them pictures. The work that I have been doing previously I call paintings. They were non-objective, before that abstract, and earlier still they were highly stylized compositions not directly concerned with representation. For more than twenty years I had preferred other qualities to those of representation.

During that time I was concerned with big abstract ideals like vitality, energy, profundity, warmth. They became my gods. They still are. I disciplined myself rigidly to work in ways I hoped might symbolize those ideals. I still hold those ideals today, but I realize that those paintings practically never, even vaguely, approximated any achievement of my aims. Quite the opposite: what the paintings told me was that I was a hard-working guy who was trying to be important.

In telling this I am purposely stressing my own reactions to my own paintings. Other people's reactions seemed to me to vary in all degrees from enthusiastic to bewildered to positively negative. All of them were influential and challenging, but none of them held a candle to the insistence of my own reactions. To me it was clear that when I aimed to fulfill the grand ideals all that the painting did was to record the vulgar gesture of a finger pointing. Was it possible that they did not want to be pointed at or were the ideals putting me inextricably in my own way?

"Gradually it dawned on me that my attention was always being drawn away from the painting and directed to the painter. The fact is I had taught myself to use the painting as a means of looking at and trying to appreciate the man that did it. This was contrary to another strong ideal which said that a man's work should be quite independent of him and possibly very much more wonderful.

. . . I have found that in accepting and immersing myself in subject matter I paint with more intensity and that the 'hows' of painting are more inevitably determined by the 'whats.' I believe that my work has become freer of arbitrary mannerisms. . . .

Great artists have always changed the succeeding tradition by giving whole new concepts to art, but I believe that they became great artists with complete naturalness and inevitability simply by painting each day for the present day's painting. I think that I, three years ago, was too much concerned with the direction that art would or might take, too much with my thoughts on the future of painting and not enough on the present. I believe that we are living at a time that over-emphasizes the need of newness, or furthering concepts.

Sure, I hate the lethargy of Mr. Average Public, but I also shudder at remembering that quite often students of mine have asked me with real bewilderment, 'What is there new that I can do? Mondrian has pushed impersonal abstraction to the absolute limit. Clyfford Still has pushed a free emotional kind of abstraction to another limit. Where can I pick up the thread?

The implication is always 'I, too, must be great.' Well, darn it, I think that greatness is a lot like sex appeal, an enviable characteristic, but a characteristic that exists in the sight of others and not in one's self. . . Painting is a fascinating, challenging and absorbing activity. My job, it seems to me, is to paint with as much completeness of energy, insight, enthusiasm, and so on as possible, and if today I feel that I achieve this more nearly by using subjects, that's what I'm going to do today. . .

The pictures reproduced here will indicate the way I am painting now. All of them are representations of definite subjects and otherwise probably not so very different from my former work. That these pictures haven't as yet had the nasty trait of mocking me has been a positive encouragement."

Park held very much the same idea in 1957, when the author talked to him in connection with the *Contemporary Bay Area Figurative Painting* exhibition organized at the Oakland Art Museum that year, the first new figurative group exhibition of any kind.

"As you grow older, it dawns on you that you are yourself— that your job is not to force yourself into a style, but to do what you want. I saw that if I would accept subjects, I could paint with more absorption, with a certain

enthusiasm for the subject which would allow some of the esthetic
qualities such as color and composition to evolve more naturally. With
subjects, the difference is that I feel a natural development of the painting
rather than a formal, self conscious one. As a person, I have nothing in
common with someone like Mondrian — he was an inventor, I am not;
I love things, and my forms come more easily out of a less deliberate kind
of invention.''[12]

(Interestingly enough, Park's reasons for resuming figurative painting were very
much the same reasons American abstractionists of the post-war period gave for
adopting *non*-figurative modes. These painters had found representation made
them self-conscious and restricted them, and they sought increasingly to be free of
all vestiges of it.[13] Park found that, for himself, figuration released deeper, more
inward and subconscious feelings, which permitted him a total absorption
in the spontaneous act of painting. What Park found by returning to the familiar,
the other artists found by pursuing the strange. Hassel Smith is a California example
of such an artist. Smith stated to Walter Hopps in 1952,

> *"I wish to feel free to appreciate* life *without relating to it, either its beauties*
> *or its ugliness. . . My paintings are intended to be additions to, rather*
> *than reflections of or upon,* life.*''*[14])

The rationale behind Park's change back to a figurative manner was, as
Fred Martin felt at the time,

> *". . . the most important act he could commit; it didn't matter how bad or*
> *good the paintings were, it was still the great motive.''*

8. M.H. De Young Memorial Museum, *David Park, Exhibition of Paintings*,
San Francisco, 1959.

9. *Contemporary American Painting*, University of Illinois, 1952, Urbana, Illinois, p. 220.

10. David Park, *op. cit.*, p. 4.

11. Alfred Frankenstein, *Art in America*, "Northern California," Winter 1954, vol. 42,
no. 1, pp. 49, 74.

12. *Contemporary Bay Area Figurative Painting*, Oakland Art Museum, Oakland,
California, 1957, p. 7.

13. Sam Hunter, *Modern American Painting and Sculpture*, New York, 1959, pp. 137-147.

14. Walter Hopps, *Hassel Smith, A Selection of Paintings, 1948-1961*, Pasadena Art
Museum, Pasadena, California, 1961.

CONTINUATION OF TRAITS

*A*lthough Park stopped painting in an abstract expressionist manner, he had been deeply altered by the abstract experience. One of the things which made his new figurative work "new" is that he brought to it a number of abstract expressionist traits. The principal ones involved paint, shape, color and space.

PAINT

In his work up through the early forties, paint itself was never the protagonist. He had carved his shapes as though he were a carpenter working a piece of wood; he would trace and retrace his drawings, changing them just a little each time: only when he was satisfied with them and had fitted them comfortably together into a pleasing mosaic would he finish them off with a coat of paint. There was little "paint quality," little impasto or surface richness.

During the abstract expressionist period, Park found that the paint itself could be the subject. He found that paint was an oozing, unstable, constantly moving plastic liquid mass whose interactions with itself produced an infinite number of transmutations of color; it was like some organic matter under a microscope; it was like life itself; it "was" life. The more paint was restricted to shapes imposed by the mind, the deader it was. The more it was let out of this cage to have "accidents" and just to be, the more spontaneous, organic qualities were conjured and the better an analogy for life and feeling it was. Paint was to be cultivated and encouraged into its own forms. The artist's victory was in understanding it and in living through it, not forcing it into submission.

This exploration of paint was a radical innovation in Park's circle and was perhaps Park's major innovation of the time. Diebenkorn was at first shocked at the way Park scooped up "terribly excessive" amounts of paint and applied them to the canvas. It was common house paint in cans, at that. The use of house paint instead of tubes of artist's colors became an accepted approach to the big canvas, but McCray and Wessels both remember Park as the first person they saw to use it. Diebenkorn said of Park's experience with abstract expressionism,

"The main thing it showed him was something about how far he could go with paint."[15]

FORMS

One of the principal traits Park acquired in his abstract expressionist period and carried over into his new figurative work was a use of natural, organic forms or shapes.

Throughout his earlier years he had forced his subjects into a mold of certain specific abstract, rather geometric shapes which were then popular with artists. There was first the famous "free form," resembling an amoeba or an asymmetric kidney bean. Park introduced it into his paintings in the guise of ponds or islands in 1935.[16] Soon after, he participated in a general tendency to develop the "free form" into a more slender, bent "boomerang" or "elbow" shape which he especially delighted to see in human figures. At first these figures were realistic and rather Bentonesque;[17] by the late thirties they were clearly cubist and related to Picasso.[18] As his paintings became more abstract, his use of these forms became more direct, less covert and rationalized, though he retained a special liking for bent elbows in his subjects.

Another form Park used was the "checkerboard" or "bow tie" shape which was popular with painters in the late thirties and forties. This was a by-product of cubism; it grew out of the distinctive intersection which was produced when two "transparent" shapes overlapped in typical cubist fashion. Park naturally used it during his cubist work of the late thirties.[19] He also created intricate overlappings in a series of paintings of abstract faces done in the early forties.[20] The particular kind of "checkerboard" triangles which came out of these face paintings became, as certain surviving drawings indicate, the basis of many of his forms in his non-objective period, though by that time these forms retain only vestiges of a cubist function or context.[21]

In the late thirties and early forties, Park used these forms to create complex interweavings of positive and negative shapes, of object and background, of line and shape. This was never more elaborately developed than in the work of that period. The cubist paintings are full of little intellectual games with form, little "conceits" which obviously pleased and amused Park and increased his ability to manipulate structural elements with virtuosity. A typical painting is *Two Figures on a Beach (no. 15)* of 1938-39?, which shows a man and a woman on a beach with the ocean in the distance. It is one great tangle of "free forms" and "elbow" shapes. Positive spaces are deliberately transmuted into negative ones. Forms seldom confine themselves to one figure; they move freely through space from one object to another. The great white "free form" is an example of both; it starts as the thigh of the figure at the left, becomes the ocean in the background and ends up as the knee of the figure on the right.

In his abstract period in the late forties, Park learned very different kinds of forms. Rather than taking forms conceived in the mind and imposing them like cookie cutters on his material, he let his material suggest the forms to him. They grew, spontaneously and organically, from the nature of paint itself. Though some of his non-objective work still contained specific geometric forms, most of it did not.[22]

When Park changed to his new figurative approach, he took this new concept of form with him. Instead of imposing shapes on his subjects, he let his subjects spontaneously generate their own shapes. He found many of his favorite forms again in nature, but now they grew out of nature instead of being superimposed on it.

COLOR

Park had arrived at a highly developed concept of the function of color almost by necessity. As he went further into abstraction in the forties, his shapes became flatter and their meaning more ambiguous. The more volume and meaning slipped away, the more color took over in the determination of space. The bottom would suddenly fall out of a shape which might have been meant to come forward; another shape which was supposed to stay back would crowd its way to the front. Suddenly these would flicker and fluctuate like optical illusions. The key to controlling these effects was color. Park found that color was more than a pleasant frosting put on top of shapes; with volume and meaning gone, color was the bearing wall, supporting the spatial structure of the painting.

In his semi-abstract work, Park had experimented with fluctuating objects and voids, turning them into neutral ambiguous, plastic stuff; color was one of his main means. He could make the "void" between two faces become a "solid" by making it dark and the faces light.[23] A "void" when painted orange would congeal almost into "solid" alongside a "solid" painted blue-grey, which in its own turn would evaporate into "void."[24] There was more than a little of the game in all this, but at its more serious level it was an exploration of what color, when free of restrictions, could do to space. Both Diebenkorn and Bischoff remember Park's emphasis on making color work. Park once told Bischoff,

> "I think you can make a thing any shape and any size and put it any place in the painting if you make it work in color."

Since only a few of the actual paintings from his abstract expressionist period are left, there being no surviving examples at all for certain kinds of paintings, according to Fred Martin, and since the rest are known only in a few black-and-white photographs, it cannot really be told for certain what he did with color during this period. Fred Martin commented on the frequent use of brilliant white areas in Park's work at this time, and said that the best of these paintings had

> "... a beautiful feeling of color — a feeling of the light being embedded in the color."

However, since Park continued at least part of the time with the same kind of shapes he had used in the profiles of 1945 and 1946, it is reasonable to think that he kept something of the same approach to color.

If color had been an ornamentation added on top in the paintings of his earlier realistic period with little spatial or expressive significance, in his abstract work it became an active, structural element in the creation of space and in the expression of attitudes. He carried this functional use of color into his new figurative painting.

SPACE

Another trait developed by the abstract expressionist movement at the school in the late forties was a distinctive concept of space which might be said to be "expanding" or "centrifugal" in character. The purpose, according to Diebenkorn, was to give the painting an exploded, expanded look of great energy. He described the technique by saying,

> *"Maybe you could put a form, a statement, in the lower left area, then pick it up again way over on the extreme right edge. This would let things expand."*

Hassel Smith says the idea was to give the impression that these forms had their "inception outside the canvas" and only confronted each other in the arena of the painting. Clyfford Still frequently developed the extreme margins of his canvases, leaving wide areas in the center blank.

Park's "centrifugal" concept of space and the intricate maneuvers with positive and negative shapes he had developed in his cubist days were both now involved in a deliberate fluctuation or play of ambiguities. Many shapes were self-contradictory, implying both positive and negative space. Some which loomed large in the foreground as they were being forced centrifugally out of the picture could suddenly subvert the whole spatial premise of the picture by switching from a positive to a negative space and collapsing, falling back through the picture, becoming a big hole instead of a protruberance. This concept was shared with other advanced artists around the school. Fred Martin stated,

> *"One of the things at the time in [Park's] work was the use of a sort of foregroundy thing which would get enormously mixed up with the background until suddenly it was all going this way (back and forth). Fluctuation — he was constantly teaching that. Shapes, colors — he was constantly doubling everything;. . . he said that things ought to be used in varying ways — this red should be used this way here and that way there. It was a big time for everybody's using ambiguities — this was the advanced thing to do. . ."*

While centrifugal, fluctuating space was common among the abstract expressionists at the school, Park was the only one who ever applied it to a figurative style. It is, in fact, one of the most distinctive personal traits in his early new figurative work.

15. See also, Erle Loran, "San Francisco," *Art News,* September 1949, vol. 48, no. 6, p. 45.

16. *Boston Common (no. 13); Summer Sports* (DP1096).

17. *Three Boys in Dunes* (DP1243).

18. *Cellist and Flutist (no. 29).*

19. *Two Flutists in Yellow* (DP1221).

20. *White Figure* (DP1210).

21. *Composition* (DP1504).

22. *Non-Objective (nos. 4 & 21).*

23. *Two Heads (no. 18).*

24. *Encounter (nos. 3 & 19).*

Part Two

EARLY NEW
FIGURATIVE ART

CIRCUMSTANCES OF
THE EARLY FIFTIES

Park's life during the first years of the fifties when the early new figurative paintings were done was very different from what it had been before. Many things about the look of these paintings reflect his personal situation at this time. He handled the novel circumstances of these years by pushing his new style all the harder.

REACTIONS TO NEW FIGURATIVE WORK

These new circumstances started with the first public reactions to his new painting. The main indication of approval for the change was the major award given to *Kids on Bikes (no. 24)* in the 1951 San Francisco Art Association annual. On the whole, though, the other awards in this annual were on the conservative side; they went to mildly abstract work; the more vigorous non-objective painting at the school was barely represented. The award hardly placed Park in the adventurous company he had kept in the three-man show with Smith and Bischoff in the same museum the year before.

Approval also came from his long-time friend, the writer Mark Schorer, who had found his non-objective work "pretty dreary," but who was elated about *Kids on Bikes*.

> *"We liked it very much. We found it very exciting and we were delighted that he had given up covering acres of canvas with non-objective work."*

A few of the artists and students closest to him who had been aware of his basic, sometimes covert, figurative tendencies — like Fred Martin and Sam Francis and to a certain extent Bischoff — had no special "reaction" at all; it was no surprise

EARLY WORK AND CUBISM

*Measurements are in inches;
height precedes width.*

14. *Mother and Child,*
1938-39?, oil on canvas,
32 x 26.

13. *Boston Common,* 1935,
oil on canvas, 29¼ x 25.

15. *Two Figures on a Beach,*
1938-39?, oil on canvas,
30 x 40.

16. *Untitled Abstract Drawing,*
1945-49, pencil on paper,
8$^1/_2$ x 11$^1/_2$.

17. *Untitled Abstract Drawing,*
1945-49, ink sticks on paper,
8$^1/_2$ x 11$^1/_2$.

STYLIZED WORK OF
THE MID FORTIES

18. *Two Heads,* 1945, oil on
masonite, 12 x 9$^1/_2$.

19. *Encounter,* 1945, oil on
masonite, 9$^1/_2$ x 11$^7/_8$.

ABSTRACT EXPRESSIONISM

21. *Non-Objective,* 1949,
oil on canvas, 34 x 25.

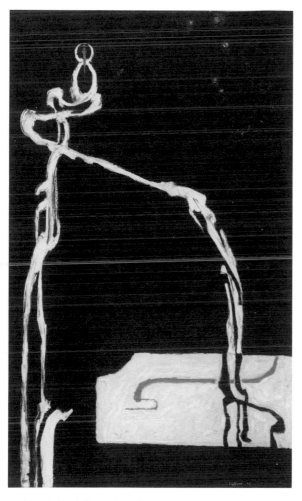

20. *Untitled* (formerly *Self
Portrait)* by Clyfford Still, 1945,
oil on canvas, 70⁷/₈ x 42.

**FIRST NEW FIGURATIVE
PAINTINGS**

22. *Rehearsal,* 1950, oil
on canvas, 46 x 35³/₄.

24. *Kids on Bikes,* 1950-51?,
oil on canvas, 48¹/₄ x 52.

23. *Portrait of Hassel Smith,*
1951, oil on canvas, 33³/₄ x 28.

26. *Still Life with Butter Dish,*
1956, oil on canvas, 20 x 16.

25. Photograph of objects
in *no. 26.*

OBSERVATION
AND
REMEMBRANCE

27. *City Street,* 1955, oil
on canvas, 59 x 45¹/₂.

28. *Two Violins,* 1936,
tempera on panel, 33 x 30.

MUSIC SUBJECTS

30. *Jazz Band,* 1954,
oil on canvas, 24 x 36.

29. *Cellist and Violinist,* 1939?,
oil on canvas, 40 x 52.

31. *The Cellist,* 1959,
oil on canvas, 56 x 56.

32. *Quartet,* 1960, ink sticks
on paper, 9 x 15 1/4.

33. *Untitled Drawing of a
Rowboat,* 1919 (age 8),
ink on paper, 1 x 2.

35. *Canoe,* 1957, oil
on canvas, 36 x 48.

34. *Canoe,* 1953, oil
on canvas, 46 x 28.

36. *The Scroll* (detail),
1960, ink sticks on
paper, approx. 4 x 6.

37. *Sunbather,* 1950-53,
oil on canvas, 36 x 46.

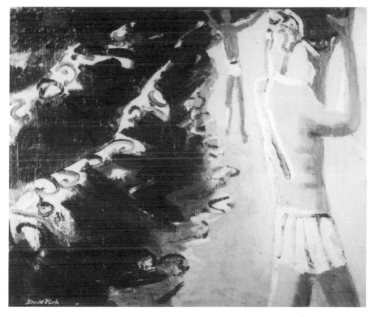

38. *Shore Line,* 1952,
oil on canvas, 32 x 38.

**DOMESTIC LIFE
SUBJECTS:
THE CARD GAME**

39. *Woman Playing Solitaire,*
1935-37?, oil on canvas,
28 x 30.

40. *Solitaire,* 1954?, oil
on canvas, 30 x 24¹/₄.

41. *Ace of Hearts,* 1959,
oil on canvas, 33 x 27.

42. *Early Portrait of R.D. (Richard Diebenkorn),* 1954-55, oil on canvas, 20 x 14.

44. *Portrait of Elmer Bischoff,* 1952, oil on canvas, 34 x 25.

PORTRAIT SUBJECTS

45. *Portrait of E. Bischoff,* 1957, oil on canvas, 22 x 20.

43. *Portrait of R. Diebenkorn,* 1957, oil on canvas, 20 x 18.

CARICATURE SUBJECTS

46. *Cousin Emily and Pet Pet,*
1952, oil on canvas, 46 x 33¹/₂.

48. *Cocktail Lounge,* 1952?,
oil on canvas, 50 x 40.

47. *Cocktail Party,* 1952?,
oil on canvas, 36 x 40.

49. *Woman with Black Glove,*
1951, oil on canvas, 26 x 24.

50. *Beach Profile,* 1953,
oil on canvas, 34 x 30.

**CONTRAST IN
EARLY NEW
FIGURATIVE
STYLE**

52. *The Bus,* 1954?, oil
on canvas, 48 x 43$^1/_2$.

51. *Bus Stop,* 1952, oil
on canvas, 36 x 24.

EARLY FIGURE DRAWINGS

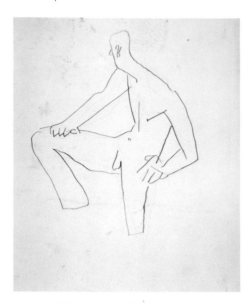

53. *Untitled Figure Drawing,*
1950-55, pencil on paper,
8 1/2 x 11 1/2.

54. *Untitled Figure Drawing,*
1950-55, pencil on paper,
8 1/2 x 11 1/2.

55. *Untitled Figure Drawing,*
1950-55, colored chalk on
paper, 8 1/2 x 11 1/2.

LATER LIFE DRAWINGS

56. *Untitled Figure Drawing,*
1955-59, black ink and red
chalk on paper, 9 x 12.

57. *Untitled Figure Drawing,*
1955-59, gouache on paper,
9 x 12.

58. *Standing Nude,* 1956,
oil on canvas, 26 x 16.

LATER SUBJECTS:
THE NUDE

59. *Nude,* 1958, oil on
canvas, 28 x 14.

60. *Drawing for "Nude Green,"* 1957?, ink on paper, 12 x 9.

61. *Nude Green,* 1957, oil on canvas, 69 x 56.

**TRANSITION
TO LATER
STYLE**

62. *Woman and Canoe,*
1955, oil on canvas,
48 x 36.

63. *Interior,* 1957, oil
on canvas, 54 x 48.

64. *Still Life with Hammer
and Pliers,* 1956, oil on
canvas, 14 x 10.

66. *Two Figures*, 1957,
oil on canvas, 36 x 29.

65. *Nude (Unfinished)*,
1959, oil on canvas,
29 x 36.

LATER SUBJECTS:
NUDES AND BATHERS

67. *Four Men*, 1958, oil
on canvas, 57 x 92.

68. *Figure,* 1959, oil
on canvas, 20 x 16.

FINAL FIGURES
AND HEADS

70. *Head with Red Collar,*
1959, oil on canvas, 19 x 16.

69. *Head,* 1959, oil
on canvas, 19 x 16.

71. *Dark Head,* 1960,
gouache on paper,
13 x 9 1/4.

**FINAL HEADS
IN GOUACHE**

72. *Head,* 1960, gouache
on paper, 11 1/2-13? x 9 1/2
(sight).

73. *Woman with Raised
Hands,* 1960, gouache on
paper, 12 1/2 x 13.

THE SCROLL

74a. *The Scroll* (detail),
1960, ink sticks on roll
of paper, 13 inches
by 31 feet.

74b. *The Scroll* (detail).

74c. *The Scroll* (detail).

74d. *The Scroll* (detail).

76. *Profile and Lamp
(Lydia Park)*, 1952,
oil on canvas, 16 x 13³/₄.

75. *Woman Smoking,* 1954-55?,
oil on canvas, 28¹/₂ x 24.

77. *Sophomore Society,*
1952-53?, oil on canvas,
38 x 46.

ADDITIONAL PAINTINGS

79. *Portrait of Lydia Park,* undated, oil on canvas.

78. *Rowboat,* 1958, oil on canvas, 57 x 61.

80. *Riverbank,* 1956, oil on canvas.

81. *Daphne,* 1959, oil
on canvas, 75 x 57.

ADDITIONAL PAINTINGS

82. *Two Female Figures,*
1957, oil on canvas.

83. *Small Head,* 1958,
oil on canvas, 11 x 9.

84. *Beach,* 1952,
oil on canvas.

to them to see Park's figurative interests more boldly expressed. This
group reacted very positively. Fred Martin said,

> *"The whole picture just shone — it was the white on the shirt of the bicycle*
> *rider; in those days the painting seemed enormous; it really seemed*
> *much bigger and much less stiff and arbitrary than it seems today."*

However, the more ardent abstractionists at the school didn't feel Park had
started anything new and significant; they felt he had faltered and fallen away
from their vanguard. Bischoff said,

> *"The heat that had been gotten up about abstract expressionism made it*
> *inevitable that anyone who switched was regarded as a traitor — a*
> *heretic. There was more of a feeling that he had 'chickened out' than*
> *anything else."*

Bischoff still calls *Kids on Bikes* "a pretty flat-footed painting; it's a sort of
outlandish, goofy thing." Diebenkorn found out about the change while
he was in New Mexico when he saw a reproduction of *Kids on Bikes* in the Art
Association bulletin.[25] He said his first reaction was,

> *"My God, what's happened to David!... Shortly after, Ed Corbett, who*
> *thought very little of David anyway, came through New Mexico. I asked*
> *him about* Kids on Bikes *and he said 'Ugh!'* [Diebenkorn felt that *Kids*
> *on Bikes] contains some of the worst stylizations David could use.*
> *I didn't like it then and I still don't like it as a painting."*

Hassel Smith said,

> *"I'm afraid that a widespread reaction to the change was that it* was *a*
> *'failure of nerve.' I have thought it was myself at one time or another."*

Neither the local nor the national art press made any comment on the new
painting, though *Kids on Bikes* was reproduced several times.[26]
Park and Bischoff, who had rebelled against the Still-dominated school
and had resigned from its faculty together, now had to pursue their careers alone
without the benefit of the school environment. At the time, they didn't even have
a common approach to art. Bischoff said,

> *"We rebelled together, but we were separated in our work."*

Bischoff moved to Marysville where he lived for several years. Park sought
a job outside the academic world to support himself and his family. He tried several
menial jobs — including putting up liquor displays in store windows — but disliked
them intensely.
At this point, Lydia Park conceived what Park called the "Lydia Park
Fellowship." She felt it was not a healthy thing for Park to be working at jobs which
seemed to humiliate him. She also wanted him to have a period during which he
could, for once, paint full-time. So, for most of the first half of the fifties, Lydia
continued her job in the University of California library, Park painted, and they lived
very simply. He now had time to paint, but his circumstances were far from ideal.
He was without the stimulation of life at the school and the many amenities and

encouragements it provided a painter. He had no regular studio; he painted in the tiny living room of their small apartment and would clean it up for use as a living room by the time Lydia came home at the end of the day.

It would have been understandable if these circumstances — the negative reaction to his first new figurative paintings, the decline of the school and the failure of his stand for Hassel Smith and the limitations of the "fellowship" years — had persuaded him he had taken a wrong path and should return both to abstract expressionism and to teaching. They did not, however. He went his new way as a painter with stubborn determination and with a certain perverse delight in being a rebel. Diebenkorn often mentions Park's "rebellious attitude" in these days and says Park was "thrilled by going way out on a limb."

25. *San Francisco Art Association Bulletin,* March 1951, vol. 17, no. 3, p. 1.
26. *Ibid.; Arts Digest,* March 15, 1951, vol. 25, no. 6, p. 10.

SUBJECT MATTER

*T*he most notable thing about Park's new work was that it was "figurative," that it involved the representation of subject matter. When he stopped painting non-objectively, Park needed another source of ideas for forms, another inspiration. He found this in representing the world he saw and knew around him. He had painted it before, of course, but he had been interested in superimposing abstract forms on it. His paintings then had been, he said,

> "... highly stylized compositions not directly concerned with representation."[27]

Now, he tried to let the world he saw give rise to forms which were stronger and more lively than the stereotypes which had come from the mind alone. He searched for forms which looked as though they could have come only from "life," not from "art." He learned to do with the representation of subject what he had learned to do earlier with paint — to cultivate it instead of forcing it to his preconceived will. Diebenkorn said,

> "He wanted very much for the subject matter to be bringing up the shape. He tried to avoid personal invention and the subjective."

Park was at first apparently very conscious and deliberate in his experiments to get his forms out of his subjects. His insistence was typical of him at the time. It can be detected in the marked stylistic differences between many of the early paintings and in a certain rigidity in carrying out his ideas, which disappeared later.

OBSERVATION AND REMEMBRANCE

During this period when representation of subject became important, one characteristic of Park as an artist came to the fore. David Park was a remarkable *observer.* He developed an ability to observe people, actions, places, things so penetratingly that he could catch and remember the essentials of something before him without disturbing even the flow of a conversation. He deliberately avoided making sketches — except in life drawing sessions — and most of the people whom he observed had no idea he was doing so. Park would then use these remembered details in his paintings days and even weeks later. He made a point of keeping it all to himself until a painting was finished.[28]

Park's ability as an observer is indicated in his portraits. He never studied portraiture, or even really tried his hand at it earlier, but in his new figurative period he became intrigued with it as one aspect of realism. However, unlike the usual portraitist, he almost never painted or drew people while they knowingly "sat" for him. He simply observed his friends and the people he saw frequently and did the paintings later in his studio. That he could get likenesses and personality by working this way is the surest sign of this special ability as an observer.

Park also worked from memories of events when he was a boy. It is not immediately obvious, but the subjects of many of his new figurative paintings are scenes from his childhood in New England.

The many boating scenes Park painted, for example, are from childhood fact, or perhaps, childhood fantasy. Boating is depicted in the earliest known work of Park's, a series of miniature drawings done for his mother at Christmas when he was eight. In one of these, the boat bears his brother's name, Richard *(no. 33).* Lydia Park believes the boating scenes go back to summer vacation pleasures; Richard Park himself, however, does not recall boating with his brother and says their vacations were usually in the mountains.[29] Whatever youthful experience or fantasy inspired it, the fondness for boating subjects appears often in his work and some of the major new figurative paintings, like *Four Men (no. 67),* * include this subject.

This almost covert use of subjects remembered from the distant past is exemplified in the painting *City Street (no. 27)* of 1955, which looks contemporary at first glance but actually mixes contemporary elements like the boy's T-shirt with elements remembered from Park's Boston youth — brick sidewalks, the lamp post, the twenties car.[30]

---

* This largest of Park's paintings was bought from the artist by the Whitney Museum through the Staempfli Gallery July 17, 1959, even before Park's first show there — a remarkably prescient purchase!

Park made no special distinction between remembered and observed subjects. They were all equally part of his image of life. He gave his paintings something of the structure of the dream, combining deeply etched childhood images with the accidents of current observation, making no distinction between them, altering and manipulating them to fit the plastic needs of the new entity, the painting. Park's freedom and lack of self-consciousness in combining these old and new subjects is a further sign of his success in doing what he said he wanted to do: "... to get in gear with those undercurrents which made art an extension of life."

QUALITY OF PLEASURE

Park's subjects and his art as a whole have one quality which is more remarkable than it might at first seem, a quality of light-hearted, innocent pleasure. It appears in his earliest work and runs through it consistently until the final period. Park's subjects are always concerned with relaxations and amusements, with what is pleasant and amiable about life. Playing music, dancing, eating, going to concerts, boating, reading, playing ball, sunbathing, napping, and the more agreeable jobs around the house like sewing and manicuring, make up his entire range of subjects.

Interest in innocent pleasures and indifference to other aspects of life was always true of Park's work. In earlier years he resisted strong influences which might have pushed him in other directions. During his mural-painting days for the Federal Arts Project in the depression, he entirely avoided social criticism. His mural for the John Muir School in San Francisco is an example. It is very much what one might have expected a young artist, still in his early twenties, to have painted for the Federal Arts Project: it is involved with labor and industry and has its share of workers in undershirts. However, it entirely lacks the bitter, specific social protest of the Mexican muralists like Rivera, who were among the principal idols of the vanguard painters in the bay area at the time, or of a local follower like Anton Refregier. One has only to think of Refregier's mural for the Rincon Annex Post Office to place Park's mural in perspective. In contrast to the vein Refregier exploited, there was also a quieter minor vein of social commentary in this period which celebrated the variety of life: different species of animals, different ages in history, stages in human life. Park's mural commemorates the joys of work and depicts different forms of constructive labor. There are workers casting metal, using a big industrial crane, building a house, digging a trench, cutting trees, and—Park's own occupations of the time—carving monumental statues and painting murals in fresco. The young men depicted at these tasks are all of a rather general type, so it is hard to impute much in the way of attitude to them, but it is obvious that they are finding pleasure and satisfaction in their employment: it is impossible to imagine any of them in a waterfront strike or a picket line.

Park continued to paint the innocent pleasures of life when he became involved with cubism. During his heaviest assimilation of Picasso's ideas at the end of the thirties and the beginning of the forties, he was never tempted to try to follow Picasso's swings from sentimentality to hostility. Park responded to Picasso's synthetic cubist paintings of musicians, still lifes, seated women and bathers scattered through the early twenties and thirties. Picasso's sentimental ballet drawings apparently did not influence Park. He was also totally unresponsive to the social issues Picasso concerned himself with in *Guernica* and related works. Only at those moments in the late thirties when Picasso himself relaxed into more genial subjects and less anguished distortions does resemblance of Parks's work to Picasso's become clear. Throughout his cubist paintings, Park's subjects are mothers and children, musicians, bathers at the beach, bathers with towels.

This same pursuit of innocent pleasure endures in what evidence we have of Park's most abstract and non-objective work. Many of the more geometric forms were derived from the face, and are sprightly and positive in character. Park's more painterly abstract expressionist work, judging from the colors and forms in the few paintings which remain, continued this quality. Writing of his own work at the time of the three-man show in 1949, the high tide of Park's non-objective work, he said,

> *"To me, a painting is a record of a state of being. An exuberant state of being naturally is reflected in an exuberant painting. It would be fine to be exuberant often and natural always."*[31]

When Park began his new figurative painting, he made an even stronger point of painting pleasant things pleasantly. He deliberately, almost rebelliously, contradicted the strident, sober, serious tone of most American abstract expressionism by pushing this pleasantness harder than he had in earlier years. Even when he was motivated by something closer to annoyance, he expressed himself through wit. Though his later subjects lack some of this innocence and become more serious as well as more solid, they are not totally removed from a certain sense of mild pleasure. This quality endures even through most of the things done during his final illness.

His friends were quite aware of this special attitude. Bischoff said of *Kids on Bikes,*

> *". . . it has a kind of 'naivete' about it. He got a wallop out of doing what he saw to be a really 'innocent' business. After the sophistication of his non-objective work and the profile things just before it, there is a real innocence to this. It was a gesture of getting down to something that was unpretentious, close to home, down to earth."*

The author remembers talking to Park in 1957 about this quality in the faces of his figures, and his admitting with a certain perverse pleasure that his figures were "kind of corny."

Park's greatest single distinction could well turn out to be that he was one of the few artists in the mainstream of his time who had the desire and the independence of mind to depict man in a world of innocent pleasure.

REPERTOIRE OF SUBJECTS

Park had a limited but enduring repertoire of subjects. Many subjects in the new figurative paintings had appeared repeatedly in the earlier pre-abstract work of the thirties and forties. Looking at the figurative paintings of the thirties and at the new figurative work, one can see differences, but one is more struck by the surprising consistencies. As might be expected, these reflect aspects of his own life.

Not all subjects were in use during any one period; certain ones would be favored, others would be entirely dormant. Every so often he would revive and re-analyze one of the dormant subjects and retire an active one. (A few subjects appeared in only one period, like the still lifes of 1956 or a series of biblical drawings (DP113 and DP1009) done in the thirties.)

Park's early new figurative subjects can be grouped under five general headings: music, life at home, beach sports, caricatures and portraits.

MUSIC

Music was so important a part of Park's personal life it is not surprising it was a frequent subject in his art. He had played piano since childhood, and wondered then whether he wanted to become a painter or a pianist, according to his aunt. He was fond of playing Bach, Scarlatti and Mozart, whom he liked for their qualities of brilliance and gaiety. Occasionally he played in duets or trios with friends like Bertrand Bronson. The Parks also regularly attended chamber music concerts. About 1949, a jazz band was formed at the school. Park enthusiastically played piano in the band, which specialized in playing Dixieland, whose bright, innocent exuberance appealed strongly to him. Douglas MacAgy played drums, Elmer Bischoff played trumpet, Charlie Clark, clarinet, Conrad Janis (art dealer Sidney Janis' son) played trombone and various others played at different times. They played for school dances, Art Association parties, Democratic Party fund-raising events and on some occasions just for their own amusement. Park stayed with the band until his back began to bother him too much to play through an entire evening. His enthusiasm for jazz and its relation to his art is revealed in a statement he wrote in 1959 for the catalogue of the Staempfli inaugural show.

> "Music is very important to me although I have too much of a single-track mind to listen to it while painting. I like to play Bach, Mozart (short piano pieces), and am quite willing to say that I render these superbly as long as no one is around to listen. And I play jazz with absolutely no competence and considerable energy with a group of amateurs who — fortunately for the 'band' — play quite well. I've grown to prefer it to playing serious music — it's a better antidote to the solitary life of painting. It has helped me in painting to be extravagant with paint."[32]

Park's circle of friends included musicians and people interested in music. Dorothy Baker, jazz enthusiast and author of *Young Man with a Horn*, was a close friend of the Parks. Charles Cushing and Bertrand Bronson on the University of California faculty were friends. When the university opened its new music building in 1958, Darius Milhaud was commissioned to do a new opera and Cushing arranged for Park to do the sets and costumes.

Music subjects appear frequently in his art in almost every period. From the earliest mature oils of the thirties there are many violinists, string trios and quartets and an occasional flutist. These same musicians continued to be one of his major subjects throughout his cubist work of the late thirties. The round shapes of the instruments and the figures countered by the lines of the bows appealed to his taste for shapes in these years. There are few musicians in his stylized work of the war years and the years immediately after, and of course, there are no music subjects in the abstract expressionist phase.

Jazz subjects are important in the early new figurative period. In fact, the first new figurative painting to be exhibited was *Rehearsal (nos. 5 & 22)*, shown early in 1950, which depicts the jazz band at the school. It is a witty painting which already has all the earmarks of his new style. Douglas MacAgy plays drums, Conrad Janis, trombone, and John Schueler, bass. Park even put a thin edge of his own head in one corner behind the piano, the closest he ever came to a self portrait in a painting. Park almost never depicted his own instrument, the piano, but there are a few exceptions.[33] Other jazz paintings occur throughout the early and middle fifties.[34] In addition to painting the band itself, Park painted the dancers they played for several times in 1953 and 1954.[35] And he painted several concert audiences about 1953 and 1954.[36]

As Park moved into his later new figurative period and had less interest in paintings based on detailed observations of everyday life, the subject of the band dropped out of his active repertoire. However, it is interesting to see that the violinists, who had been absent from the scene throughout the time of the band subjects, begin to reappear.[37] The last major oil he was able to complete was a large painting of a seated woman musician, *Cellist (no. 31)*, done in 1959. At least five of the works on paper in his final period are of violinists; one is a flutist. Park had a loyalty to his earliest subjects which is surprising when one considers how much his work as a painter and his tastes in music changed.

In these paintings, the motif of clothes becomes almost a symbol for "outer self," for superficiality, pretension and a certain hardness and lack of inner feeling. In *Cocktail Party (no. 47)* and *Woman with Black Glove (no. 49)*, both from about 1952, a rather similar woman is presented in this way. In *Party*, her bright green dress, her furs, her red hat with veil covering the eyes, her earrings and her black glove holding a martini glass all fail to disguise her. She is a square, middle-aged woman with a thick neck and a jut-jawed, graceless face whose only discernible feature, her over-ample mouth, is covered with an excessive red rectangle of lipstick. In *Black Glove*, a red hat with a picket fence of veiling across the eyes, a green dress and a black glove frame a flat, blank face.

Two other paintings of this period, *Cousin Emily and Pet Pet (no. 46)* and *Mother-in-Law* (DP547), also caricature the pretensions of middle-aged women, the most frequent target of these satires. Cousin Emily — an imaginary cousin — in her coat, fur, adornments, obscured by her hat, walks a disagreeable little Pekinese, whose name is French slang for "fart," under the awning of an apartment house entrance. *Mother-in-Law* is actually of his mother-in-law, though the sarcasm is gentler. According to Lydia Park, it is

> "... so typically an old lady, bright hat and collar and lace. He was caricaturing my mother... and people with their outer selves on. He used to be amused at her Victorian attitude that you must always look nice."

In these caricature paintings, Park not only uses the motif of clothes, symbolizing superficiality, to get his point across; he alters his usual manner to react expressionistically to the subjects. Color is deliberately clashing and discordant. A bright red against a bright green — like a cheap Christmas ornament—and black dominate. Most interestingly, the linear contours change. Instead of the simple, sweeping curves and the clean contours found in *Kids on Bikes* and in most of the early new figurative works, the contours in *Cousin Emily,* for instance, are deliberately fussy, broken, lacking in tensile strength or rhythm.

Woman Smoking (no. 75), of 1954, seems to be the most hostile, least sympathetic of the caricature paintings. It depicts an attractive but aggressively talkative woman who has a brutal red impasto skid of lipstick for a mouth, too much jewelry and a cigarette held elegantly in a hand with blunt red nails. It is of an artist and patron acquaintance whose behavior had annoyed him. Diebenkorn said,

> *"He felt it to be a cruel painting; he didn't sign it or exhibit it."*

Park's urge to do sarcastic caricatures was related to his interest in portraiture. But caricature was more than a means of releasing his feelings about particular people or situations. It was the farthest point in his aggressive, almost belligerent search for a new source of forms within a realistic approach to subject matter. According to Diebenkorn,

> *"He wanted very potent, very demanding subject matter; he wanted to bite. He wanted very much for the subject matter to be bringing up the shape; he wanted something to make these colors come out sharp and hard—so he tapped this area of his reaction to people."*

PORTRAITS

It is not surprising that Park's iconoclastic search for realism in subject matter should lead him to paint portraits, even though the portrait as a type of painting was in disfavor with the more progressive painters and though he himself had never done portraits before. What was particular about the human face now concerned him more than what was general, or ideal, and hence too "artistic."

People in his immediate circle of friends and acquaintances interested him most as subjects. He painted his wife, he painted his artist friends, he painted other people on the faculty at the school or the university and their wives and children. Quite often, the subject was given the portrait as a surprise gift. Many times, a painting would only incidentally be a portrait. Lydia Park is faithfully depicted in many paintings which were not specifically designed as portraits, as occasionally are his friends, the Bakers, or the musicians in the band.

He liked painting people whose personalities he could observe casually over a long period of time. Often what impelled him to paint a portrait of someone was not the desire to depict their total appearance or personality, but only to show some special aspect of it. When he painted *Phyllis Diebenkorn* (DP1033), he presented her in a surprisingly austere manner. When she commented on this, Park told her with amusement, according to Diebenkorn,

> *"I see this thing in you that lots of other people don't see, and that is your puritan soul."*

The portraits which were most works of art were those he did of the painters who were close friends. *Portrait of Hassel Smith (no. 23)* was one of the earliest new figurative paintings. It was painted in Park's small studio at the school. Smith says he didn't exactly pose for it, but he did have a habit of visiting Park in his studio during the lunch hour and he was aware Park was painting it. Park worked on it for a long time. There is much of the caricature about it. Park presents Smith with a bald pink head, a garish sport shirt, with a great claw of a hand lifting the butt of a cigarette to his pursed lips. According to Lydia Park,

> "It's very much his friend Hassel in one of the wild shirts he used to wear. The hand is even a Smith hand, not just a Park hand — he always had paint on his fingernails. And this pink was no mistake. Hassel, if he got a little flustered or sunburned, would turn pink."

The general sense of color and various little stylistic mannerisms also tie this in with the other caricatures. It was, of course, a sympathetic one, and it reflects the relation between these two painters. Both had a dry, sharp wit. Bischoff said,

> "David's reaction to Hassel as a person was a matter of great innate sympathy. They both shared a much more immediate response to things, a connectedness with actuality — and they both had a sense of humor."

Park painted Bischoff and Diebenkorn on several occasions. He did two of each in his early new figurative style, one of each in his later style.[39]

The contrasts between the early and later portraits are so great that one has a strong sense of two different styles. In the earlier ones, there are still shapes with carefully cut contours, filled with rich but flat paint. The composition and use of space is asymmetrical and perhaps a bit forced. The faces are innocent, open, naive. In the later ones, the heads are larger than life size. They emerge directly as heavy volumes out of a layer of rich paint. There are no edged contours; noses and mouths are all great pieces of paint laid on boldly and calligraphically. Where the earlier paintings are boys painted boyishly, the later are mature men painted in a bold, masculine manner.

The portraits of painters not only reflect their appearances and personalities, sometimes they reflect a little of the painters' own styles. The glasses Hassel Smith is wearing are painted with an elegant linear gesture which is typical of Smith but not like Park at all. The later portrait of Bischoff has a certain sober ponderousness, a certain red-blue-purple richness which is like a painting Bischoff did of himself.

DOMESTIC LIFE

The second grouping, subjects of domestic life, consist mainly of women around the house. Many of the new figurative versions of this subject are from 1952 and 1953. They show a woman, often recognizably Lydia Park, manicuring her fingernails in her dressing gown, sitting by a lamp, working at a sewing machine, reading a newspaper or a book, writing. These scenes of domestic life are, for the most part, nocturnal, lamp-lit subjects, reflecting evenings in their small apartment during the "Lydia Park Fellowship." Though Park did not paint in the evenings, he was interested in observing Lydia at her various after-dinner occupations. These paintings are full of the actual properties, the furniture and clothes of the time.

The earliest of the new figurative paintings of women at home stay very close to subjects actually observed. However, within a few years, Park broadened his subjects to include material remembered from his past. Examples are *Solitaire (nos. 2 & 40)* from about 1954, and the later *Ace of Hearts (no. 41)* of 1959. The woman in *Solitaire* is not Lydia Park, and the subject comes not from anything Park was apt to have seen in the fifties, but from his remembrance of his family life in New England. On summer evenings, members of his family would sit around their vacation home reading and playing solitaire; in later years, Park's mother played solitaire every evening, Lydia Park recalls. An undated painting which appears to have been done in the mid thirties, *Woman Playing Solitaire (no. 39)*, is further evidence of the persistence of his subjects. The 1954 painting is almost an exact repeat of this earlier composition. Though the character of the paint and the color are very different, the position of the figure, the head leaning on the elbow and the other arm outstretched to the semicircle of cards on the table are very much the same.

Another domestic subject was a group of people seated around a table drinking or eating. This subject was quite popular in American art in the thirties when Park began using it. It is the one social realist subject which agreed with Park's taste for innocent domestic pleasures. He approached it without any desire for social comment or criticism. It also gave him an intricate, compact group of figures to work with. (The earliest known use Park made of this subject was in *Four People Drinking Wine* (DP1206). When he resumed figurative painting in 1950, one of the earliest paintings was *Table with Fruit* (DP18), showing three people around a table set with glasses, cups and a bowl of fruit. *Cocktail Lounge (no. 48)*, listed as 1952, with its drinkers crowded around a table, also falls into this category. *The Table* (DP13), of 1956, a painting of brown faces and brown wall against white shirts, tablecloth and dishes, is a version of this subject which moves toward some of the ideas of the later period.)

Looking at these paintings of domestic life done in the first half of the fifties, it is impossible to tell which ones were from actual observation, and which ones were remembered from his boyhood past. He painted a kind of timeless, continuing life in which family women and their quiet tasks and pleasures endure like archetypes.

BEACHES AND BOATING

Beach sports and boating are consistent subjects in Park's repertoire. It was already mentioned that his earliest known drawings, done when he was eight, show boating scenes, and that often in the new figurative work he recalls memories or youthful fantasies of boating. Beach and sport subjects were dormant during most of the thirties. (The only exception is *Football Game* (DP1225) of about 1936 or 1937, an intricate, foreshortened aerial view of a stylized tangle of football players.) In the new figurative work of the early fifties, the sports depicted are entirely associated with the beach — boating, beach ball, swimming, sunbathing. In the later new figurative period there are countless beach scenes, boating scenes and nude bathers.[38] These beach figures merge gradually into the nudes of the later paintings. In his final period, when he returned to re-examine subjects which had interested him in earlier years, one of the last oil paintings he started was a great magenta and black scene of figures reaching up for a beach ball, *Boys with Beachball* (DP80).

In music Park took an active role, but in sports he was a spectator. It is easy to understand how Park would be sympathetic to music subjects, harder at first to understand why he would be interested in subjects involving sports. Park's subjects, though, were much more apt to be what he saw, not what he did; they depict others, not himself. In spite of his interest in portraits and in painting people close to him, Park seldom did a true portrait or even a caricature of himself (one exception is *no. C*). As he said, ". . . a man's work should be quite independent of him and possibly very much more wonderful." Park had an ingrained dislike for anything "narcissistic" in his art; he made every effort to avoid self-consciousness, to achieve a submersion of ego, an absorption of self in painting. The very fact that he was *not* an active sportsman made this subject all the more available to him as a painter.

CARICATURES

An exception to Park's usual approach to subject matter occurs in a group of paintings which can be called caricatures. Surveying Park's subjects, it can seldom be said that the manner in which he painted was highly conditioned by strong feelings about particular subjects. Except for a certain general pleasure in the human figure and in people, Park avoided reactions to subjects strong enough to affect the manner in which he painted. His student, Tom Holland, asked him about "social comment" painting. Holland said,

> *"He didn't like it at all. It was usually obvious; I couldn't even get him to talk about social comment painting. He disliked painting as a comment. He always wanted a very neutral kind of use of the figure, not a commentary or message. [If a painting showed, say, a man playing a cello, to Park]. . .this wasn't a comment on someone playing the cello or something like that — it was just a painting and that is all it was."*

In the caricature paintings, Park's emotional reactions do noticeably condition the manner of painting. These caricatures, which are truly expressionist, constitute his farthest reach in his pursuit of realism in subject matter. Some were done as early as 1951, but most are from the years 1953 to 1955.

Though he generally painted people with affection or at least sympathy, he approached them in the caricatures with barbed hostility and witty ridicule. They are never deeply angry and especially never lacking a certain wry humor, but their critical intent is unmistakable. He would emphasize what was fallible and vain in the people who were his targets by stressing the clothes and makeup and cocktail party smiles they used to create a flattering image of themselves, yet he revealed that underneath this false exterior they were dull and ugly.

27. David Park, *The Artist's View,* September 1953, vol. 6, p. 4.

28. Lydia Park and Richard Diebenkorn interviews. See *Profile and Lamp (no. 76); Manicure* (DP15); *Butterdish (no. 26).*

29. Richard Park — note to author.

30. Lydia Park interview, comment on *no. 27.*

31. Erle Loran, *Art News,* "San Francisco," September 1949, vol. 48, no. 6, p. 45.

32. Staempfli Gallery, *David Park, Recent Paintings* (exhibition catalogue, New York, New York, 1959, no page numbers).

33. *Practice* (DP1253), about 1953, and *Woman at the Piano* (DP45), signed 1954.

34. Other early jazz paintings are *Band* (DP1007) of 1951, *Jazz Band (no. 30)*, perhaps 1952, *Dixieland* (DP1027) of 1956 or 1957 and *Jazz Band, Trombone* (DP1074).

35. *Jitter Bugs* (DP1502), *Dancers (no. 8)*, *Sophomore Society (no. 77)*, *The Dance* (DP7). These paintings, too, have a predecessor; there is a *Dancing Couples* (DP1239) which must be from the mid thirties.

36. *Concert* (DP38) and *Audience (no. 6)*.

37. There is one *Violinist* (DP516), dated 1957.

38. Among the beach sport scenes are *Shore Line (no. 38)*, *Beach Profile (no. 50)*, *Sunbather (no. 37)* and three titled *Beach (no. 84, DP1065, and DP1008)*. The boating scenes include *Four Men (no. 67)* and *Rowboats* (DP1072) and many others (DP17, DP21, no. 34, no. 35, DP507, DP512 and DP1257).

39. The early ones of Bischoff are *no. 44* and DP1079. The later one is *no. 45,* probably 1957. The early ones of Diebenkorn are *no. 42,* perhaps 1955, and DP1031, about 1954 or 1955; the later is *no. 43,* also probably done in 1957.

STYLE

Subject matter and realism were never the most important things in Park's new figurative venture. The aesthetic essentials of the work of art itself were always his first concern. Several aspects of Park's early new figurative style deserve close attention: his use of contrasts, of mosaic compositions and expanding space.

Park's attitude at this time was decidedly iconoclastic — he deliberately set out to be an "image breaker." The somewhat defensive nature of the circumstances of his personal life helped push him to the creation of aggressive contrasts in his art aimed at destroying conventional concepts and accepted canons of style of all sorts. Park himself said,

"Your job is not to force yourself into a style, but to do what you want. . ."[40]

According to Diebenkorn,

"He had an utter disdain for the New York school because he felt New York put style absolutely first. . . . it was a kind of anti-style thing. He felt that style was a threat to individuality."

USE OF CONTRASTS

Park not only rebelled against non-objective painting; he also used ideas he had acquired during his non-objective years to attack many previously accepted ideas of earlier figurative art. Park's chief means of attacking older images and asserting his own new ones was an aggressive use of contrast. In the handling of any formal element — shape, color, light, texture — he deliberately challenged the usual notion of balance. Most paintings have big shapes, middle-sized shapes, small shapes; they have bright tones, middle tones and dark tones. Park made the thick things thicker, the bright things brighter; he made the thin things thinner and the dark things darker; he simply left out most of the rest. He literally pulled the picture apart.

Most early new figurative paintings reveal this aggressive use of contrast in one way or another. It is perhaps more "programmed" in the earliest ones, but it is quite discernible in works up to 1957. It appears in the first widely known new figurative painting, *Kids on Bikes (no. 24)*.

Beach Profile (no. 50) is a good example of this contrast operating at many levels. The painting, apparently from 1953, shows a ponderous, massive profile of a woman pushing out of the picture in the foreground and a skinny stick figure of a man and his shadow on the beach in the background. This enormous chunk of foreground figure is entirely out of scale by more traditional canons. Such a figure appears in almost all the early new figurative paintings. The thin stick figure is also frequent. There are precedents in Picasso for combining both stylizations, though whether or not Park knew of these is another matter.* There is also something of Piero della Francesca in such colossal figures.

If he took ideas learned from abstract expressionism and used them to attack conventional canons of figurative painting, he also did the reverse. He revived older figurative devices to attack some of the more sacred tenets of abstract expressionism. One of these tenets was that the picture plane is to be stressed, that it is not to be broken by assertions of deep space. Park directly assaulted this notion. When an amateur enthusiast of abstraction disdainfully accused him of "breaking the picture plane," he later fumed and, according to Diebenkorn, said,

"Ridiculous! I'd like to break the damn picture plane!"

Park had two devices to break the picture plane and create a deep space. One was the use of large foreground figures against small background figures. The other was a diagonal converging line moving rapidly back into the picture. This line has many rationalizations. Sometimes it is a fence,[41] sometimes it is a piano keyboard.[42] It can be a trombone,[43] or the oar of a boat[44] or a path.[45] However, these devices are used in such an exaggerated way that they seem almost deliberately unconvincing. They overstate their case to such an extent that they become more of a rebellious gesture symbolizing deep space than an effective spatial structure; in spite of the gesture, Park still stayed largely with the abstract expressionist respect for the picture plane. Diebenkorn commented on Park's

* See Alfred H. Barr, Jr., *Picasso: Fifty Years of His Art,* New York, 1946. These contrasts run throughout the early work in this style. *The Woods* (DP19) pushes the highlights of sun on leaves to an absolute white, the shadows to an absolute black. It also has perhaps the most massive chunk of outsize foreground figure of any of these paintings. *Audience (no. 6)* puts an enormous single profile against a texture of heads. Even the red and green forms of *Kids on Bikes (no. 24)* are organized around this principle.

"rebellious attitude in busting up the picture plane" by saying,

> "He liked the long reach back, as in Velasquez' Las Meninas. It would be
> David's thrill to bring one figure way, way forward and to take a long
> reach in. He would sort of get on me for respecting the picture plane.
> I would sort of prick his balloon by saying, 'You're not the rebel you think
> you are — you do respect the picture plane."

There is little question, though, that Park made a rebellious assault on it,
whether he went all the way or not.

THE EXPANDING SPACE DEVICE

While Park was in the abstract expressionist movement at the school, he gave his
forms and space a sense of being expanded or exploded. In his early new figurative
work, he applied this device to subject matter. One object or group of objects will
slide out of the picture at the bottom, creating a kind of magnetic attraction across a
great void in the center to forms which have nearly disappeared out of the picture at
the top or the sides. *The Bus (no. 52)* of about 1954 and *Interior (no. 63)* of 1957 are
good examples. In both, windows are oddly elevated to the tops of the pictures
while the human figures thrust downward, forward and outward at the bottoms of
the pictures. Park used this device with the same disrespect for previous figurative
conventions and the same rebelliousness and aggressiveness which marks much of
the first new figurative work. In some of the first paintings he goes to really forced
extremes, though he does it with style and wit. *Portrait of Hassel Smith (no. 23)*
has a thin sliver of shapes down the left side which, upon close examination, turns
out to be an open window with the view beyond. The fragment of a self portrait
in *Rehearsal (nos. 5 & 22)* is another extreme. When the origin of this device is
considered, it is quite apparent that these first new paintings are very knowing, very
witty — and very ruthless figurative parodies of the school's standard abstract
expressionist style. Park in later works seldom made such extreme, outlandish use
of this device, but it remained one of his favorite techniques throughout the early
new figurative period. In fact, it is one of the last devices to give way to the changed
point of view in his later work; it is clearly present as late as 1957 in *Interior.* (It is
also nearly Park's alone. Diebenkorn quit abstract expressionism, for one thing, to
escape this kind of composition.[46] Bischoff made little use of it at any point.)

MOSAIC COMPOSITION

Park developed a technique of composition, a sort of mosaic or jigsaw puzzle
device, which had a significant unifying effect in his early work of this period. Park
needed some such device; his aggressive use of contrasts and expanding spaces did
not easily make a unified composition; the contrasts were, in fact, difficult to keep
within bounds.

Park exercised this control by making certain that all elements in his
pictures, no matter how diverse and contradictory in relative size or color they
might be, were definite, clean cut shapes, and that these shapes were rigidly locked
into position in a single mosaic pattern. He made everything — kids, bikes, women,
beaches, walls, bathers — such controlled, consciously thought out shapes. His

compositions, as eccentric as they are at times, are as tight as a typesetter's locked form of type. Because of this rigid control these paintings are able to contain a far greater saturation of contradictory elements than would otherwise have been possible.

Park had ground rules for putting these mosaic compositions together which helped him control the contradictory elements and turn them into a homogeneous plastic material.

First of all, in most of the early new figurative work — *Kids on Bikes* and *Beach Profile* for example — he eliminated both a horizon line and a ground line. The background of the painting is often simultaneously floor, wall, sky and then suddenly just the flat paint surface of the picture plane. Many of the figures stand in an uncertain "somewhere" with unspecified connections to the space they occupy. In spite of his equivocal attempts to assert space by contrasting big foreground figures with small background figures and by using a receding diagonal line, this elimination of horizon and ground lines so weakens the orthodox structural architecture of figurative space that most of his shapes become a vague, changeable substance which is thing, space and surface all at once.

Park further unified his shapes by making his "solids" suggest "voids" and his "voids" suggest "solids." The huge head and neck of the woman in *Beach Profile* is so plain an area, and the beach and waves in the background are so intricate, that one might want to read the profile as "void" and the background as "solid" if it were not for other cues. The same is true for *Cocktail Party (no. 47)* and a number of other paintings.

The way paint is applied unifies the mosaic compositions. Everything is painted with the same broad stroke and the same opaque paint. There is no atmosphere; a face is no more detailed than the pattern of a floor; near and far objects receive almost equal treatment; everything has the same impasto surface.

Finally, Park used the fall of light to rationalize and integrate his shapes. In the thirties and forties he had used a series of conceptual, abstract shapes like the "free form." In his non-objective work he discovered the spontaneous shapes which developed out of a free use of paint. Now, in his new figurative work, he continued with something like these spontaneous shapes, but he rationalized them so that they appear to have been caused by the nature of the subject itself, not by the artist. There is no longer the feeling that these shapes are in any way non-objective. They give the appearance of being the natural result of the fall of light — they are "explained" by it. He had occasionally used this device before — as early as the Piedmont High School tapestries (DP1101), and was to make it one of the main techniques in his later new figurative work, but it is in this period that he gives it its first clear statement. For example, this technique can be seen in two paintings from 1952, *Profile and Lamp (no. 76)* and *Beach (no. 84).* In both cases the faces are broken into patterns of irregular bands and shapes which appear to be highlights and shadows caused by the intense light of the lamp in one case, the sun in the other. Diebenkorn noted that Park's

> *". . . intense highlights and shadows give him a sort of naturalistic sanction for the kind of plastic volumes he had done more abstractly earlier."*

At its highest development, this mosaic composition of shapes becomes what Diebenkorn once called ". . . a kind of fabric of persons." Park found one of his inspirations for this in the work of Piero della Francesca, particularly the crowded group of figures in the fresco of the Queen of Sheba and her court, and Mark Schorer recalls his admiring the rhythm of the horses' legs in the *True Cross* fresco. As one might expect, Park responded to the linear contours and the carefully cut negative spaces. Beyond that, however, Park found the frescoes a model for his mosaic-like compositions. Portions of one figure are laid over those of another, creating nearly abstract shapes which can be arranged rhythmically. In the little open spaces between, bits of other figures — perhaps only a forehead and an eye — are seen, adding additional abstract shapes. This great piling up of positive upon positive and positive within negative truly creates "a kind of fabric of persons," Park's furthest development of the mosaic of abstracted objects and spaces.

The most directly Piero-like painting, though not the most elaborate mosaic, is *Heads* (DP1091). A large foreground head cuts this long, narrow horizontal painting at top and bottom. The space to the left of the head in the middle is almost entirely filled with the third head. There is also a certain slow grace to the largest head which is reminiscent of Piero; this head, and Park's frequent use of a motif of sloping shoulders and forward-stretching neck, both have overtones of Piero, but this apparently was the limit of Park's interest in Piero's particular kind of figure.

The paintings of jazz bands and dancers done from 1952 to 1954 seem to develop this mosaic composition, this "fabric of persons," to the furthest point. *Sophomore Society (no. 77)* pulls many harshly contrasting patterns and differently colored faces into a pattern of contour against contour in which a central negative space contains portions of dancing couples in the distance. Perhaps most interesting in its handling of subject is *Jazz Band (no. 30)*. The entire painting is positive against positive, figure against figure, with the exception of a few tiny chinks of background at the top. The three horn players stretch from side to side and top to bottom. In the tiny spaces left between them Park wittily puts the head of the drummer in one case, his drums and drumsticks in another, and the keyboard and hands of the pianist in a third.

COLOR

One element which helped determine Park's style in the early new figurative paintings was his concept of color. In his non-objective phase, he discovered and explored what color could do to the space of a painting when volumes and meanings were taken away, and only patterns of shapes were left. When he began painting figuratively again, even though he was still strongly involved with shapes, these shapes naturally had representational meanings and a certain amount of volume again. As a result, color could no longer be the main dictator of space. However, it was still a very positive element.

Park had a certain notion of color which runs through most of his work from the earliest things we know to the last. He generally worked with a "full palette" of color. He was different from many contemporary artists like Tomlin, Gottlieb, Guston, Still and Rothko, who work up a "color scheme" for their paintings by using only a few colors or by leaving out certain colors altogether. Other artists work with a full palette — Hoffman, Gorky and de Kooning, for example — giving the feeling that they reflect the total orchestra of color, even though they each achieve a certain individual balance.

Park probably preferred these full palettes partly because they resisted being absorbed into decorative color schemes. The very limitations of paintings based on limited color schemes make them reach out sympathetically to related colors in the surrounding environment, while fuller palette paintings tend to be complete in color within themselves and to resist this tendency to be absorbed in some scheme beyond their boundaries. "Art ought to be a troublesome thing,"[47] Park said once in this context, not a decorative thing, and he painted representationally in these colors partly to make his paintings more immune to the effects of decor.

Park did occasionally work with color concepts other than the "fuller palette." At the beginning of the new figurative work he tried strong, garish color contrasts of reds and greens and blacks and whites.[48] He also did a number of one-color paintings, most in the mid fifties. There are "yellow" paintings, "blue" paintings, "red" and "green" paintings.[49] They do not seem monochromatic, however; Park generally succeeded in using the fall of light or the natural tone and color of the subject to rationalize the single color character. He often built deliberately around the three primaries. There are many red-blue-yellow or red-green-yellow paintings in his oeuvre.*

* Among the examples which could be pointed to in the more cubist works of the late thirties and early forties are *Two Flutists in Yellow* (DP1221), *Football Game* (DP1225), *Cellist and Violinist (no. 29)* and *Woman in Striped Robe* (DP1241). The profile paintings of the mid forties go strongly to greys and oranges, but many, including *Encounter (no. 3)* and *Two Heads (no. 18)*, have elements close to all three primaries in them. This continues into the new figurative period. *Cocktail Lounge (no. 48)* puts red, blue and yellow accents against grey. *Cocktail Party (no. 47)* counters large grey masses with red, green and yellow, and *Flower Market* (DP20) combines red and yellow with both blue and green. In the later new figurative works the same full palette and emphasis on the primary trio continues and can be found in paintings like *Small Head* (DP64) and *Head with Red Collar (no. 70)*. The final works also have this: the great *Head (no. 13)* and *Face with Hand on Eye* (DP1205) are examples.

40. *Contemporary Bay Area Figurative Painting,* Oakland Art Museum, Oakland, California, 1957, p. 6.

41. *Kids on Bikes (no. 24)* and *White Fence* (DP1200).

42. DP45, DP1253.

43. *no. 30.*

44. DP17.

45. DP53.

46. See *Contemporary Bay Area Figurative Painting,* Oakland Art Museum, 1957, p. 7.

47. *Ibid.*

48. *no. 46,* DP547, *no. 49, no. 51,* DP18.

49. DP56, *no. 52,* DP34, DP70, DP38, DP53, DP1 and others.

Part Three

LATER NEW FIGURATIVE ART

CIRCUMSTANCES OF THE LATER PERIOD

Midway in the fifties, Park's new figurative style went through a drastic evolution: by the end of the decade it had become a very different thing from what it had been at the beginning. This evolution had its own internal, purely artistic reasons but it was conditioned by Park's changed personal circumstances in these years.

The circumstances of the early fifties had been isolated, insecure, defensive. In contrast, the later fifties were the most fortunate years of his life.

COMPANIONS IN FIGURATIVE PAINTING: BISCHOFF AND DIEBENKORN

For one thing, Park acquired allies and companions in his new figurative painting. At first he had no other artists to share his new point of view and the group around him at the school was unsympathetic to his new work. This altered when Bischoff and then Diebenkorn also began a kind of figurative painting. Both Bischoff and Diebenkorn were impelled by their own inner reasons, but as they themselves changed, they came to appreciate the courage and merit in the change Park had made. In turn, Park found their pursuit of this new direction very stimulating. He had always been a rather gregarious painter used to working in rapport with other artists, and he had been largely without this closeness for several years. Now the three became close companions in the new figurative venture. They had life drawing sessions together, they got together over coffee to talk about and criticize their current paintings, and they and their families did many other things together. The companionship of two artists as able and challenging as Bischoff and

Diebenkorn helped Park sharpen and heighten his work and emboldened him to paint in more of a grand manner, abandoning some of the rather limited and rebellious devices of his early new figurative work.

The public began to regard the three as constituting some kind of new group or movement. Park alone doing this sort of painting made it merely an idiosyncrasy; three well-known artists doing it gave it the status of a potential new direction, a possible new style.

Bischoff began figurative painting in 1952. He and Park had left the school over the Hassel Smith issue that year. Bischoff also separated from his wife at the time. He left Berkeley to live in San Francisco and went to work driving a truck for Railway Express.

> "It was a great upheaval for me. Sometimes these breaks that one makes come concurrently, everything at once."

He was ready for a change in his painting, too. He felt abstract expressionist painting, which he had been doing for six years, was "playing itself dry."[50] Bischoff said he had been "straining, trying to get some sort of character" in his work.

> "I think it was a reaction to the aridity of the non-representational world in which I had been working. In representational painting you have a tremendous range of response to call up. . . The first thing I did was landscapes. . . I started to make life drawings and drawings sitting in the truck lunchtime, looking in cafeteria windows. I was tremendously keyed up and I felt these stupid, simple things of people sipping a cup of coffee were really loaded. . . . It was not so much an excitement about a form as an excitement about the heart of the matter."

Bischoff felt that in his change to new figurative painting,

> "Park was a very important influence. The influence was of the total person and what he stood for, and the demands he made of himself, but this is not the whole story; if I didn't like the painting I wouldn't have responded to the person. Whenever I visited Dave, seeing his paintings was a stimulating and enlivening experience for me."

Bischoff went to Marysville in the fall of 1953 to teach at Yuba College. Park would occasionally go to see him there, and Bischoff visited the bay area. Bischoff moved back to Berkeley in the summer of 1956 and was invited to rejoin the faculty of the California School of Fine Arts, which in the meantime had settled again into a progressive but also more stable pattern, and he had a major exhibition of his new figurative work in the school gallery that year.

Bischoff's figurative work was similar to Park's in some ways, very different in others. Like Park, his early things generally depict some ordinary observed situation—a woman reading in bed, a figure on the beach, young men in front of school buildings. Bischoff's forms had been, at first, more cubist in their angularity and chunkiness than Park's, but he moved toward smooth lights and atmospheres with gradually changing tones and shades of color and other effects outlawed under the cubism he had learned at the University of California. Bischoff's distinctive use of these effects gives certain of his paintings a strange poetry, a poignancy and nostalgia which are quite absent in the blunt directness of Park's work. In the late fifties when both began doing nudes, Bischoff made frequent use of a classical reference which almost never entered Park's work.

Richard Diebenkorn had committed himself to new figurative painting by 1955. He was younger than the others — eleven years younger than Park. Although he had been Park's student at the school after the war, he had become by far the most celebrated painter of the three. His distinctive abstract expressionist work had just been given a major one-man show in New York and he had been in demand for some time on the college circuit as a visiting artist and teacher.

Diebenkorn changed to a new figurative style because he had come to feel there was much about abstract expressionism which was basically alien to his temperament. In 1957 the author wrote of Diebenkorn's attitude:

> *". . . a growing mistrust of what he feels is a certain flamboyant emotionalism led him to seek a new channel of development toward a more restrained, held-in kind of impact in figurative painting."*

Diebenkorn explained his feelings about it to the author in an interview in 1957.[51]

> *"I came to mistrust my desire to explode the picture and super-charge it in some way. At one time the common device of using the super-emotional to get in gear with a painting used to serve me for access to painting, too, but I mistrust that now. I think what is more important is a feeling of strength in reserve — tension beneath calm. I don't want to be less violent or discordant or less shocking than before; but I think I can make my paintings more powerful this way."*

Interestingly enough, Diebenkorn's change was largely unrelated to the early phase of Park's new figurative work. He was away from California in these years and what little he learned of Park's change only distressed him. He was more responsive to de Kooning's work in this period; when he learned several years later of de Kooning's abandonment of abstract expressionism for a sort of new figurative manner, he was much more deeply affected. He came to know of de Kooning's change in 1953 through articles like Thomas B. Hess' "de Kooning Paints a Picture" in *Art News.*[52]

> *"My faith in abstract expressionism was shaken when so strong a man as de Kooning had changed. I began to do some fooling around with it [new figurative painting] even while I was at Urbana."*

Diebenkorn taught at the University of Illinois in Urbana in 1952 and 1953. In the fall of 1953 he returned to California and began seeing Park again, who showed him his new work, including things he had just exhibited in his King Ubu show. Diebenkorn said of the things he saw in 1953,

> *"I can recall feeling that somehow this was the wrong kind of realism; it seemed pre abstract expressionist. It involved a literalness I thought was wrong. . . . This looked bad for representation to me. What de Kooning was doing had more hope in it, I felt, but David just brushed off any consideration of de Kooning. You couldn't talk to him about de Kooning's work; he wasn't going to be caught dead seriously considering it."*

Park and Diebenkorn did not really have any close bond in their work until about 1955, when Diebenkorn himself became more directly involved with new figurative work and Park began moving from his early into his later new figurative style. It is this later style, beginning about 1955 and 1956, which Diebenkorn admires in Park's work.

The interchange of ideas and influences between Park and Diebenkorn — among all three, in fact — was a complex one. Occasionally, as in the case of still-life paintings, the exchange could go back and forth several times; certain paintings of Diebenkorn's could inspire Park to revive and redirect earlier ideas of his own which had been the inspiration for Diebenkorn in the first place. Of greater importance than matters of influence and counter-influence, however, is the respect each had for the other and the stimulation they found in each other's company.

Diebenkorn's work had certain special characteristics within the new figurative range which differ from Park or Bischoff. He had a much slighter involvement with what he would call the "genre" aspects of figurative work. True, in his smaller oil studies he had done portraits, still lifes and landscapes which depict the particular, but in his major paintings he operated on another level. Where Park's work was almost totally concerned with the human figure, in Diebenkorn's case environment, with or without human presence, was at least as important. His landscape background, his porches, windows, sunlights and shadows accurately reflected the mood of the environment seen from the Diebenkorn house in the Berkeley foothills down across the Berkeley-Oakland lowlands to the bay beyond, or in later years the mood of the Los Angeles scene. The houses in Diebenkorn's paintings were halls of mirrors, full of shifting, kaleidoscopic rectangular planes and voids. Their rectangularity was unique among the works of these painters and their sense of space was a reminder that Diebenkorn and John Hultberg, who had a similar vision, had worked together in San Francisco. This quality was especially apparent in Diebenkorn's early new figurative work. An observant reviewer, speaking of this quality in his first new figurative show, said,

> ". . . reproduction gives a false idea of the original. It fails to give the creepy feeling of yawning space. [His] paintings. . . seem to turn aside into mirrors, or fall into windows, or change into paintings within paintings."[53]

Of the three principal figurative artists, Diebenkorn was certainly the greatest virtuoso with color and with the handling of the brush. The cool brilliance of his blucs and purples, his greens and yellows was achieved with a kind of sour simplicity and contempt for skill which only someone of great natural technical ability could afford.

During the later fifties, all three were teaching in art schools. Gradually, younger painters interested in their approach developed out of their classes and by 1957 there were over a dozen painters painting seriously in something of a new figurative manner. This group of friends and students gave Park an environment which was very different from what he knew in the beginning of the decade.

RECOGNITION FOR PARK

Park's circumstances were also improved by the recognition in exhibitions and reviews which he was receiving at an increasing rate by the mid fifties.

At first, Park was ignored or bypassed in the reviewers' columns, though oddly enough, his first new figurative paintings were reproduced prominently in the same journals without comment.[54] However, the gradually increasing appearance of Park's work in exhibitions helped establish his name and his work with the public.[55]

Park was invited to show in the big University of Illinois biennial in 1952. In 1953 recognition increased. The bay area *Arts Digest* reviewer, the writer and poet Lawrence Ferlinghetti, singled out Park and Bischoff in the association annual and recognized them as painters

> *". . . who have gone through abstract periods and are now producing objective-expressionistic work. [He spoke highly of their]. . . deeply subjective expressions, with color and form that succeed in creating the sensations of abstract paintings."*[56]

Park had his first one-man exhibition of new figurative painting in August 1953 at the King Ubu Gallery; he got a brief but good review from Alfred Frankenstein. After noting the sameness of much local abstract expressionism, Frankenstein said,

> *"This. . . may help to explain why an artist like David Park, recently a devotee of the freest kind of non-objectivity, has returned to the subject in his current show. . . at their best, they combine a grandly massive and monumental handling with swiftly improvisational drawing and a subtly selective palette."*[57]

Most of the paintings in the King Ubu show were reproduced in the special Park issue of *The Artist's View*.[58]

Park had a one-man show at the Paul Kantor Gallery in Los Angeles in 1954: Kantor, who also exhibited Diebenkorn and Bischoff in this period, had been attracted by the "German Expressionist" quality of Park's caricature paintings. Park also received another award at the association annual of 1954.

The Richmond Art Center, under the direction of Mrs. Hazel Salmi, gave Park a comprehensive one-man show in August and September 1955. This same year, Park's *City Street (no. 27)* was included in the very selective exhibition of West Coast art organized for the third biennial of Sao Paolo, Brazil, by Dr. Grace L. McCann Morley, director of the San Francisco Museum of Art. It was shown several times in San Francisco and illustrated as a result of the biennial.

In 1956 Park and Diebenkorn had a total of eleven paintings purchased by Walter P. Chrysler, Jr. for his collection.[59] This unusual event was given much coverage in the local press and taken as a higher order of success than previous, less spectacular honors.

In 1956 Park had a small one-man show at the College of Architecture, University of California, and also won an award in the Oakland Art Museum annual. Bischoff was given a major one-man show, the first of his new figurative work, at the gallery of the California School of Fine Arts in January 1956 in celebration of his return to their faculty. Diebenkorn had a one-man "Guest of Honor" show at the Oakland Art Museum that year and received other honors.

The first exhibition concerned with new figurative painting as a whole was organized by the author, in response to suggestions by Glenn Wessels and Fred Martin, and presented by the Oakland Art Museum in September 1957. It subsequently was shown at the Los Angeles County Museum and the Dayton Art Center. The paintings of Park, Diebenkorn and Bischoff were featured, but other artists, many of them students of one of the three, and all selected by them, were included as well. The other artists were James Weeks, a contemporary rather than a student who had consistently painted figuratively without any abstract interlude; Joseph Brooks; William Brown; Robert Downs; Bruce McGaw; Robert Qualters; Walter Snelgrove; Henry Villierme and Paul Wonner. Nathan Oliveira should have been included in the exhibition but was not. Fred Martin was on their list and was invited, but declined the invitation.

The question of a new figurative movement was at least raised, if not answered, by this exhibition. Its catalogue, written by the author, as Thomas Carr Howe, director of the California Palace of the Legion of Honor, said,

> "... came to be regarded as a kind of basic bible in which the tenets of the new faith are clearly set forth."[60]

It prompted the first major article on "Figurative Painters in California"[61] in the national press. Park also had a "Guest of Honor" exhibition at the Oakland Art Museum and was included in the University of Illinois biennial again in 1957.

Honors continued to increase. In 1958, Park won an award in the San Francisco Art Association annual again, exhibited in the Richmond, Virginia, Art Museum quadrennial and in *Art USA* in New York City. This was also the year of Diebenkorn's first one-man exhibition of figurative painting in New York City at the Poindexter Gallery. In 1959 the De Young Museum in San Francisco gave Park a one-man show. He was boldly selected by George Staempfli to inaugurate his new gallery in New York in September 1959. *Time* illustrated one of his paintings in color, along with a Clyfford Still and, in its own breezy fashion, recognized Park as the sire of a new school.[62] He was naturally included in a spate of shows on the return to the figure, including Indiana University's *New Imagery in American Painting* and the American Federation of Arts traveling show, *The Figure in Contemporary American Painting,* both in 1959. In 1960 he won a major prize in the joint Pennsylvania Academy Annual-Detroit Institute biennial, with *Three Bathers* (DP505) which was illustrated in the *New York Times.*[63] Other honors and attentions increased up until his death in September 1960.

Park was prepared to paint and to paint the way he wanted whether he was a "success" or not, but gradually, success came to him. George Staempfli said,

> "He once told me that he had painted so long in California, and had so little recognition, that he had reached a stage of being completely resigned to the fate of painting... for years out there, selling an occasional painting, teaching and remaining known only on a local scale. When the show in New York... was a great success, David... was deeply pleased and rather surprised."[64]

APPOINTMENT TO UNIVERSITY FACULTY

In the last half of the fifties, Park also enjoyed the kind of professional status as a teacher which he had long deserved. He was invited to join the faculty of the University of California art department in 1955 and served as an associate professor until his death. The university was quite a contrast to the California School of Fine Arts. The school in the late forties had been a giddy, heady, unstable place, full of excitement and new ideas, poor salaries and capricious shifts in favor. This yeasty turbulence had its points but it had its problems.

    The university art department's salaries and faculty circumstances were infinitely more desirable, even if its student body was less adventurous. It was also then just a little slower than the California School to pick up new ideas. Back in 1949, when Park and Bischoff and Diebenkorn were all teaching at the school, they had put on one of the area's first extreme abstract expressionist shows. The leading figures at the university art department were tolerant, but they regarded the show and the kind of painting in it with considerable caution and hesitation.[65] By the time Park joined the faculty, abstract expressionism had become the core of the department's thinking. That the faculty wanted to have one of the new figurative painters in the department is an indication of its desire for a broad range of viewpoints and its early recognition of the significance of this new painting. Park was considered for an appointment even prior to 1955. James McCray was one of those most responsible for advocating Park, as were Glenn Wessels, Karlk Kasten and Herschell B. Chipp. In the midst of this abstract-expressionist camp, Park, according to Glenn Wessels,

> "... took the attitude of being the loyal opposition. He reserved the right to be independent of the dominant ideas of the faculty, though he concurred with others."

    Park as a teacher is a subject which could be explored at length, perhaps by his former students. It might at least be noted, however, that what he taught at the university was a figurative kind of art, based on drawing and painting the nude.

    Some of his pupils have already become notables. One of them is Sam Francis, who had been injured while on duty with the armed services. While recuperating in a local hospital, Francis asked if he could be instructed in painting. A request for volunteer assistance was sent to the School of Fine Arts and Park responded. He taught Francis to do small, dark abstract watercolors. Later, Francis studied at the university.

    The salary and the security of the new university situation made it possible for the Parks to buy a small but very attractive redwood house on a Berkeley hillside favored by other university faculty members. It had a big studio on the top floor with a skylight and a fireplace and a view of the bay in the distance through redwood trees. The greatest number of Park's new figurative paintings were done in this studio. During a sabbatical leave, he painted here almost constantly. Many of Park's friends had been university faculty people even before his own appointment. After 1955 this was increasingly so, though they were apt to be people outside the art department, like the Mark Schorers or the B.H. Bronsons.

    The circumstances of the later fifties — the companionship of Bischoff and

Diebenkorn, the growing public recognition for his work and the security of a position on the university faculty—all had their effect on Park. He became less belligerent, felt less that he had to prove a point. His art became more mellow, more relaxed. He no longer conceived his art as a rebellious campaign against existing standards. He immersed himself in the fabrication of broadly felt, richly painted images of the human figure.

50. *Contemporary Bay Area Figurative Painting,* Oakland Art Museum, Oakland, California, 1957, p. 9.

51. *Ibid.,* p. 12.

52. *Art News,* March, 1953, vol. 52, no. 1.

53. "L.C.", *Reviews and Previews, Art News,* vol. 57, no. 1, March 1958, p. 13.

54. *Kids on Bikes (no. 24)* not only appeared in the *San Francisco Art Association Bulletin* (March 1951, vol. 17, no. 3, p. 1) but in *Arts Digest* (March 15, 1951, vol. 25, no. 6, p. 10). *Manicure* (DP15) (Alfred Frankenstein, *San Francisco Chronicle,* "This World," May 31, 1953, p. 17) and *Bathers* (DP1517) (Lawrence Ferlinghetti, *Arts Digest,* "San Francisco," May 1, 1953, vol. 29, no. 15, p. 7) later received similar ambiguous treatment.

55. See page 117-118 for list of exhibitions, 1952-1960.

56. Lawrence Ferlinghetti, *Arts Digest,* "San Francisco Annual," February 15, 1953, vol. 27, no. 10, p. 12.

57. Alfred Frankenstein, *San Francisco Chronicle,* August 15, 1953, p. 24.

58. *The Artist's View,* San Francisco, California, September 1953, no. 6.

59. *Oakland Tribune,* June 21, 1956, and elsewhere.

60. Thomas Carr Howe, "Foreword" to the catalogue, *David Park, Recent Paintings,* Staempfli Gallery, New York, 1959, p. 7.

61. *Arts,* December 1957, vol. 32, no. 3, pp. 26, 27.

62. *Time,* November 9, 1959, pp. 80, 81, 83.

63. *New York Times,* Sunday, November 29, 1959, p. 21.

64. Undated letter to the author.

65. Erle Loran, *Art News,* "San Francisco," September 1949, vol. 48, no. 6, p. 45.

SUBJECT MATTER

*D*evelopments in Park's art during the fifties were so great that one cannot help but find the early and later new figurative works to be of an entirely different character. The changes within his new style were so considerable, in fact, that it might be said they were as great as the changes he made going into, or out of, abstract expressionist painting. These can again be seen both in the subject matter and the style of his work. In his subjects he moved from a genre realism to that most ideal of figures, the classic nude. The change in his style is a little more difficult to describe so patly; it could be said that it involved the emergence of an illusion of light conjured out of paint.

An examination of his paintings in chronological order reveals the necessity of some kind of distinction between "early," "later" and "final" new figurative work. While the material could conceivably lend itself to different subdivisions, these three, in the author's opinion, seem to be the most logical and natural.

There is no specific date which one can give to the change from "early" to "later." The first characteristic of the "later" period is the use of the nude, which begins in 1955. The last characteristic of the "early" period to disappear is the expanded or exploded space, which crops up intermittently until 1957. Thus, the "early" period is 1950 to 1955-57; the "later" period is 1955-57 to 1959. The "final" period, conditioned by his terminal illness, is 1959-60.

STILL LIFES OF 1956

Although the major subject of his later work was the nude, Park did have a momentary adventure with still life in the summer of 1956 which is worth mentioning first.

Both Diebenkorn and Park explored this subject about the same time. Diebenkorn did small still lifes of bottles, scissors and other simple objects when he first began painting figuratively again. His immediate inspirations were the still lifes of Manet, but he also recalls having very much in mind earlier teachings of Park, who had his students practice by doing one quick drawing after another of a simple object — a hammer, a pitcher, a hand. When Park saw Diebenkorn's little still lifes,

Diebenkorn said he "was delighted and wanted to try them too." No surviving paintings indicate Park had ever done a still life before, though he had done objects on tables as part of a larger scene, like *Table with Fruit* (DP18). Now he tried painting simple objects around his house—the sink in his studio, a little cloisonné bowl Lydia Park used as a butter dish, a hammer and pliers, a cup and saucer, a hair brush and comb.[66] Though they were carefully observed, they were actually painted from memory. The paintings are all broadly, lavishly painted in spite of their very small size, often hardly more than a foot square. The great scale of the brush strokes becomes a very vivid part of their impact; they are almost like tiny fragments of an enormous mural. The shapes are no longer clean-cut contours; now they are simply heavy swaths of paint.

Bischoff commented that the still lifes exemplify Park's emerging later style. Speaking of *Still Life with Hammer and Pliers (no. 64)* specifically, he said,

> *"The interrelation of these things falls on the color and the light and the volume, not on the contour. The background shape is not a shape any longer, but a dumb, blunt shape, Van Gogh-ishly clumsy as compared with a Florentine grace of contour. Where I like David's things most is where I feel their coherence was through painterly means and not through the locking together of patterns."*

These still lifes introduce another characteristic of the new figurative paintings, especially those of Diebenkorn and Park—the tendency to choose either very large or very small sizes. The small paintings go down to less than a foot square in Park's case and even less than six inches square in Diebenkorn's. Park used the small size primarily for still lifes and portrait heads. Diebenkorn, always more interested in environment, used them for these and also for little cityscape or "housescape" studies which are generally more directly realistic than his larger works. In his larger works, he once said, he felt an obligation to make a more developed, considered statement. He did not carry over the manner of his smaller studies because

> *"It is hard to believe anyone would want that much undigested realism."*[67]

Park had done big and little paintings before in the late forties. In contrast to the enormous paintings and drawings of those days, some of which reached nine feet, Fred Martin recalls he once exhibited a whole show of tiny abstract landscapes about the size of a sheet of typing paper at a small gallery in Sausalito, in summer or fall of 1949.

After the group of still lifes in 1956, he never did another, though there continue to be many still life objects in his paintings of the next few years—like *Boy Painting* (DP1102)—and these are painted with an obvious enthusiasm for their potential of color and texture.

THE APPEARANCE OF THE NUDE

Externally, Park's revival of interest in the nude was connected with his taking up life drawing again. He had taught life classes in the early days at the California School of Fine Arts and did so again when he began teaching at the university in 1955. He also took part in life drawing sessions organized by small groups of artists.

Bischoff, William Brown and Paul Wonner had a few life sessions as early as 1953 before Bischoff moved to Marysville. Park's early *Portrait of Elmer Bischoff (no. 44)* was based on drawings done during one of these sessions, begun again in the mid fifties at the suggestion of Diebenkorn, who had enjoyed similar sessions when he taught at the University of Illinois in Urbana in 1952 and 1953. They were held generally in Park's studio after 1955, though on occasion they took place in other artists' homes or studios, and became more spasmodic after 1956.

Park's new interest in the nude was more than a response to the availability of live models. It was a change in attitude. When he began painting in a new figurative manner, he was trying to get away from what he felt to be the confinement of abstract art. He turned his back on art forms bred from other art forms, on classrooms and studios and much of the typical world of the artist. He plunged into the pursuit of forms which came directly from what he could see in the life around him or remember from his youth. As he came to terms with the artists' world again, it began to reappear in his paintings. Where before he painted figures which were as far removed from the art world as possible, now he painted the nude figure, the model, a being who exists only in the realm of art.

The nudes of the later period go through a brief evolution from bathers to true studio nudes. The bathers and beach figures Park was doing in the mid fifties all have a certain plausibility about them — they look as though they actually had been observed or remembered in ordinary life. The first nudes are simply these same bathers and beach figures without swim suits. Park once told the author, and Lydia Park confirmed the fact, that some of these figures alternated between swim suits and nudity several times. Park never totally abandoned the swimsuited figure even while he painted nudes. The earliest known nude is *Woman and Canoe (no. 62)*. Dated 1955, it depicts a girl bather thigh-deep in a stream, holding the end of a canoe. She is very close to being pretty — Park's people are often at their most attractive in these years — and her young breasts are made conspicuous by the fall of light and shadow.

Nude bathers appear frequently for a while. In river or pond scenes of 1956, like *Riverbank (no. 80)*, several figures sit or stand along a bank, perhaps with a tree in the background, while others stand in the water. These begin to recall certain compositions of Puvis de Chavannes and Renoir and a familiar but imaginary world which exists only in paint, more than they do any bathing scenes Park could have witnessed. Others from 1956 and 1957 have a quality of an ocean beach about them, with golden sand in the foreground, blue surf and sky beyond.

Certain figures begin to be obviously derived from life models, and the bathing scene rationalization diminishes by 1956 and 1957 as in *Bathers on a Beach* (DP16) of 1956 and *Two Female Figures (no. 82)* of 1957. The first known painting frankly to depict a model is *Standing Nude (no. 58)* of 1956, in which a pony-tailed girl who also appears in many of his life drawings is shown standing before the red brick fireplace in his studio. The celebrated painting, *Nude Green (no. 61)* of 1957, presents a model with her hand on a chair. Another standing *Nude (no. 59)* of 1958 recalls the figure against the fireplace of the year before, but she is now transmuted beyond a particular model into a general woman and painted in a rich, forceful way.

As the nudes based on life models begin to appear, it becomes clear that Park's nudes are related to certain traditional types, but totally unrelated to others.

Park's nudes might be said to follow a "life" or "studio" tradition, based on the use of actual nude models, often depicted in the setting of the studio. There is nothing of a more classic tradition: there is no sense of canons of proportion derived from antique sculpture, no knowing continuance of specific poses associated with certain artists like Polyclitus or Michelangelo, no mythological or allegorical subject matter.*

Park's figures reflect another characteristic of the studio or life model tradition; they avoid any overt sense of the erotic. In his paintings and perhaps more significantly his private life drawings, he accepts the genitals directly, frankly, without subterfuge and yet without special concern. He was interested in the total physical body and his response in the largest sense did not lack sexuality. However, he was not an artist anxious or eager to deal with erotic subjects. He responded deeply to the physical rhythms and structures of the body, but without making an issue of its eroticism.

Park's figures eventually begin to transcend their life studio origins and go beyond the level of the merely naked into the more ideal realm of the nude. No longer does the viewer ask whether they are bathers or life models, whether they are clothed or naked. Clothes assert the social personality and deny the animal, physical organism; mere nakedness does the opposite, asserting organism, denying personality. Park's nudes unify personality and organism again; they are members of that ideal race which exists only in the imagination and on the painted canvas, in which flesh and spirit are again one.

There are many paintings from 1957 on in which these transcendental figures, this union of person, light and paint occur. A very good one is *Two Figures (no. 66)* of 1957. Like almost all the later nudes, its figures stand rather than sit or recline. Against a dark grey-blue background that is vaguely like an ocean, a man and a woman are caught in a late afternoon shaft of sun. The woman heads toward the foreground, already partially out of the picture, turning her head back toward the center. Deeper into the picture, a full figure of a man is seen from behind. The two have no sense of communication with each other, but the lines of the arms, with their typically prominent elbows, and their paired poses pull them together. The blast of light cuts shapes and contours within the figure of the woman which are unexpected, but seem plausible. Her entire front is a white plane of light, but her

---

* There are a few exceptions in which some more classical elements appear in Park's work. During the Federal Arts Project, he did a frieze of Bacchic dancers for the music building at Mills College (DP1518). He also designed muse-like figures, dressed in classical chitons, for the handsome tapestries in the Piedmont, California, High School (DP1101) at that time.

There is at least one special canon of proportion which occasionally interested him. It is a certain manner of foreshortening which makes the legs and lower torso, and the draperies covering them, larger, and the head smaller. This first became fashionable in the last half of the fifteenth century in the work of Botticelli, Pollaiuolo and others, though Park could have picked it up from a much more modern version, perhaps even figures like *Esquire's* "Varda girl." Park consciously derived the long, forward-sloping neck of his figures from Piero della Francesca.

face and neck are entirely in shadow except for a thin crust of illumination. A great shadow between arm and torso cuts a clean, positive contour. Bits of brilliant color blaze out of the shadows, giving them an unexpected electric charge.

Park's friends were aware of this transcendental quality in his later figures. In Diebenkorn's opinion, the early new figurative things had been,

> ". . . a kind of extension of the American representational tradition, a kind of genre thing. There had to be a rationalization for the presence of the figure. The earlier bathers had to be doing something. They would be romping, playing ball, drying themselves with a towel; it was a kind of reason for the bather. At one point he was able to throw this off and his figures began to simply exist on the canvas. After the transition, the towel became much less important and the rationalization disappeared."

Phyllis Diebenkorn observed that,

> ". . . in the last couple of years he was making a more philosophical effort to pull everything together. The nude was the best way to do this because it takes the figure out of the regular and ordinary. He didn't just want to do a particular, specific person; he had to make it stand for more, and the nude was the best means to do it."

---

66. The still lifes are: *Still Life with Butter Dish (no. 26), Still Life with Hair Brush* (DP71), *Still Life with Pitcher* (DP76), *Still Life with Hammer and Pliers (no. 64), Still Life with Cup of Coffee* (DP78), *The Studio Sink* (DP1064) and *Sink* (DP1032).

67. *Contemporary Bay Area Figurative Painting,* Oakland Art Museum, 1957, pp. 11, 12.

STYLE

*I*n the later new figurative paintings, subject was not as important to Park as style. He had given a lot of attention to the development of the nude from 1955 on. By the latter part of the decade, he had studied and painted it often enough to be increasingly casual about it. He ceased to look for new ideas about the subject aspect of the figure; his attention was on the style in which he painted it.

The paintings in which his figures reach their transcendent quality are a curious interplay of light and paint. While light and paint alone have specific qualities which can be very limiting and confining for the artist, Park worked them together into a kind of plastic unity which gave him remarkable freedom.

THE ROLE OF LIGHT

Light is the special catalyst which gave Park the freedom to manipulate the various elements in his late work. In a typical painting of this kind, a strong blast of illumination, like a spotlight or a ray of late afternoon sun, falls on and almost overwhelms the figures, which nearly dissolve into random planes of white light and dark shadow.

Park used this fall of light, and the highlights and shadows it made, in an abstract, structural way. While he could not overtly distort the figure without losing the sense of plausibility and realism he wanted, he could manipulate highlights and shadows within these harshly lighted figures with considerable indifference to "fact," yet not disturb the viewer's sense that the figure was lifelike. Sometimes the more accidental and unexpected the highlights and shadows were, the more real and lifelike the figures seemed. In the thirties when Park first began putting abstract shapes into his work, even the simplest shoved their way into the viewer's consciousness. In the late fifties, Park used an infinitely greater number of abstract shapes, but, by means of this device of strong light and shadow, he made them stay within the limits of what appeared to be real and plausible.

Park's resultant liberty to use abstract forms was considerably greater than might have been expected in a figurative style. In fact, the illusion of plausibility which this kind of light and shadow gave him is so strong it can even carry along a few things that are deliberately *not* plausible, like the red-nosed face in the foreground of *Four Men (no. 67).*

COLOR AND PAINT

Park used this liberty to develop certain paint and color qualities even further than he had before. He achieved an effect of great lavishness, painting with broad, crusty brush-loads of pigment. He laid these on with a willingness to accept the "goopy, sensuous" accident of shapes and texture, since almost anything could still be made to seem convincingly figurative. Most often, there are two principal elements, a warm, light flesh-yellow-white range, contrasted against a dark cool blue or green. Frequently, there are red highlights, or red lines occasionally substituting for black lines.

At moments, his color sparkles with totally unpredictable little jewels of pigment which are among the principal delights to be found in these works. A painting like *Figure (no. 68)* of 1959 would photograph strongly in black and white, but this would leave the viewer totally unprepared for the brilliant glitter of the blue-yellow-red stripe on the hip, the orange ear, the turquoise and green shadows and the other flecks and frosts of oranges, reds and greens which float like faceted stones in this great lather of paint. Park's use of the fall of light not only rationalizes the abstract shapes within his figures; it seems also to account for these brilliant, unexpected bits of color.

LIFE DRAWINGS

Much of the style in these later figure paintings is the result of explorations which took place in the medium of drawing and were only painted on canvas after the ideas were well crystallized in Park's mind. Certain qualities of the drawing medium itself went along when the idea was transferred. There are perhaps three hundred working drawings of one sort or another. By comparing large numbers of slides of Park's paintings with the portfolios of drawings, the author has been able to identify with certainty which sketches Park used for some of his paintings. This has thrown considerable light on his processes.

It is startling to find that each of his figures is not only a shape or a series of shapes—it is a set sequence of strokes. In each of the variations he drew, Park not only changed the proportions of the shapes involved, he experimented with the strokes which create them. For example, the line which indicates a pectoral muscle may continue down the inside of the arm in one version; in other versions of the same pose, it continues into the line which indicates the back. It is almost as though he were creating characters in oriental calligraphy, in which the order and sequence of the strokes determine the meaning of the character. In *Interior (no. 63)*, for example, and in the series of preparatory drawings which he did for it, the curve of the man's face goes directly into the curve of the neck of the T-shirt. Each version is different in some way, but such calligraphs as this one for the neck recur unchanged. One sequence of drawings in which he experimented with related but different calligraphs for the union of the arm and the pectoral muscle is illustrated *(nos. 53, 54 & 55)*. Numerous other calligraphs of this sort can be followed from drawings to paintings.

It is remarkable how minor and subtle the changes are in the sequences of Park's drawings. Once he decided on a pose, it remained basically unchanged through all its variations, which sometimes extended over a period of several years. Even the order of strokes remained the same. Park would lavish infinite effort in refining it. He combined it in group compositions now with one other separate figure, now with another. But he did not change it. This is totally in contrast to Diebenkorn's way of working,[68] where the transmutations are infinitely greater and more kaleidoscopic.

In the later drawings, there is no longer any difference between "line" and "shape." The insistence on contour and the hard, unvarying wire line of the pencil in his earlier work disappears. He uses brush and washes of India ink. The brush line is thick and thin: in one place it will be a line in the true sense; in another it will be a great blob of shadow, a shape in itself. Moreover, there is now a variable grey instead of one tone of lead black. There is almost always a feeling that the contour outlines have opened up to register the fall of light on the figure.

Bischoff points out that in Park's later work he ceased to be interested in patterns of elegant linear contours and became concerned with lines and shapes more directly derived from his brush. Park learned to carry the casual spontaneity of the drawings over into the paintings, and they too become "paint" more than they do "line" or "shape."

Other aspects of Park's way of handling paint in his later paintings derive from drawing. He was fond of creating intense shadows and highlights in his paintings, which he often actually painted in black and white, using colors only in the intervening values. This came largely from the black and white of his ink wash drawings.

Sometimes the process of translating a drawing into a painting accounts for certain special nuances. The well-known painting *Nude Green (no. 61)*, for example, has heavy dark lines and shadows within the figure, but no lines separating the figure from the background, which is intriguingly inconsistent. The life drawing on which it is based has black lines creating the outer contour of the figure as well as forms and shadows within. When Park translated this drawing into a painting, he kept the internal dark lines but eliminated the outline since the change of color between background and flesh was enough to establish the contour of the figure. The result is to make the painting one step more removed from the expected and conventional than the drawing is.

The paint quality of these later figures also owes something to the life drawings. In the drawings, Park developed his ability to be free, broad, spontaneous in his approach, to be a little heedless and indifferent about the specific result, to let splashes of ink, footprints and doodles accumulate on them. Like private conversations, they are relaxed; there is little concern about what is good enough or bad enough; the only real fault would have been to be forced or unnatural. Park learned to carry this casual spontaneity of his drawings over into his paintings. He was increasingly able to paint a face in a couple of fast, effortless strokes, accept the results and leave them alone.

As Park did more of his late figure paintings, the distinction between the preparatory study and finished painting vanished. He was no longer apt to translate a specific drawing into a painting. He developed an immense repertoire of remembered poses, whose basic calligraphic strokes he could do directly on the canvas from memory. The paintings finally become a combination of preliminary drawing and finished painting all at once. They have the broad, black lines of the life drawings; they have the intense highlights, though these in paintings have to be applied by brush, where in the drawings the white paper sufficed.[69] It can be seen from the final uncompleted oils like *Nude with Towel* (DP44) how Park unified painting and drawing into a single act; how he drew with the brush, then painted with the brush, and further drew and painted; how he refined the figure from the image in his mind through the various layers of paint to the final surface in one sequence.

68. Herschel B. Chipp, "Art News from San Francisco," *Art News,* September 1956, vol. 55, no. 5, p. 18 and "Diebenkorn Paints a Picture," *Art News,* May 1957, vol. 56, p. 44ff.

69. *Ethiopia* (DP543), *Les Baigneuses* (DP539) and *Daphne (no. 81)* all exemplify this phase.

Part Four

FINAL NEW FIGURATIVE ART

*L*ife for Park during the last year or so of his life was dominated by a losing struggle against back illness which was finally diagnosed as cancer. He continued to paint in oil as long as he could still get up the stairs to his studio and move to his easel. When he could no longer paint upstairs, his friends made him a makeshift easel which he could use sitting down in the living room and he painted a great many remarkable gouaches. It eventually required a considerable physical effort to paint; he would paint for a few minutes, then rest, and paint again. After the last operation, he could no longer sit up to paint; he turned to ink sticks on paper.

He worked as much as his strength would allow, and continued to work until very near the end. It is not given to every artist to have one of those rare and exalted final periods of accomplishment. For some, death is sudden and unexpected; for many, the spirit has declined before the flesh begins to fail. And not every artist has the courage to pursue his art in the face of the ultimate odds. However tragic Park's suffering and his early and disquieting death are, there is at least the consolation that the momentum of his work was not only sustained, but, in a way, increased.

PAINTINGS WITH HEADS AS SUBJECTS

There are several special groups of paintings from this final period, one of the most stirring being a series of heads. These begin in oil in his later period and reach their fullest expression in the gouaches of his final period. These heads, often solitary, ocasionally two or three together, have a monumental quality and are carved out of great gobs of paint with a wide brush. As action painting, they are as free and spontaneous as any abstract expressionist work; as image, they do something more.

In painting the face, every slight change in line, every variation in a fleck of paint, triggers off whole new sets of ideas about the personality behind the face. It is easy for the painter to be relatively free in his handling of subjects like trees and mountains; however, few painters can, or even try to, paint the face with real boldness. Back in the late forties, Park had constructed abstract designs based on the head. Now, in these late works, it is a particular sign of Park's mastery of his art that he could achieve insight and a directness perhaps beyond that of any other American artist in painting this subject.

These late heads grew out of his portraits. The 1957 portraits of Diebenkorn *(no. 43)* and Bischoff *(no. 45)* already showed Park's ability to take up slab-like brushfuls of paint and to maneuver them against each other in tight quarters at high speed, catching the flare of a nostril, the blink of an eye as they sweep across the canvas. *Small Head (no. 83)* of 1958 started out as a portrait but went its own way into paint and beyond likeness. Though there are occasional heads from as early as 1957, the most compelling heads were done in 1959. They no longer have anything to do with portraits. They appear to have emerged directly on the canvas and are not based on drawings in the way many of the nudes are.

Some of the 1959 heads have blunt, black outlines, a technique carried over from his drawings. Now, however, these wide lines function more as shadows, falling behind or beside the head. Where these black shadows occur, so do glaring highlights, the result of strong shafts of light burning into the picture, bleaching the normal colors of these heads into unexpected hues and shades, cutting unpredicted abstract shapes and forms within them. The blasts of light are the key; they make the heads look plausible, the volumes look real, the incredible licenses in paint and color seem inevitable.

One of the finest of these paintings is called simply *Head (no. 69)*. The canvas is about a foot and a half square, the head is larger than life and crowds the canvas. Ponderous black tracks of paint outline parts of the head, suggesting not only shadow but hair as well. Half the face is a white facet of light; the other is a heavier brown-red body color. This head has a tremendous directness about it. There is something of Park's innocence of spirit in it, yet the enormous, smouldering black shadows in which the eyes are hidden give the head a cast of sadness and poignancy. There is an alarming depth to its monumental humanity, covered over with a reassuring brilliance of color and paint. One is tempted to think of certain works by Rouault, though Diebenkorn says Park

> *". . . would not have been flattered to be compared with him. He regarded Rouault as over-subjective and self-pitying."*

Other heads among these late oils have an equal brilliance, but more strangeness than depth to them.[70] Some of the last gouaches achieve heads which combine both strangeness and depth. *Dark Head (no. 71)* is like a giant Byzantine negress whose face looms forward, transfixing the viewer with a stare which implies knowledge of other realms of being. *Head (no. 72)* also manages a direct gaze but is timid, uncertain, wounded looking. *Woman with Raised Hands (no. 73)*, however, has the same monumentality and compassion as the oil *Head (no. 69)*.

A special sensation comes when the late heads and figures are compared with the earlier ones. The earlier figures have a physical, corporeal quality more than they have feelings, emotions or personalities. This was in part inherited from the mural figures of the thirties, in which abstract forms were stressed while character and personality were minimized. To some extent, this is a common characteristic of the nude in western art, which constitutes a heroic, ideal race, aloof from mortal passions, like the mindless, heavenly birds of oriental painting or the angels of Baroque art. In the last years, though, in the presence of the reality of disease, suffering and death, Park's figures stir into wakefulness and consciousness; they descend into the arena of human feeling and become an expression of Park's own struggle with mortality. Arising from their most inward regions comes a quiet but powerful awareness, manifest through their increasingly deep, direct gaze. It hovers somewhere between the serenity of the ideal and the anguish of the mortal, in a visionary, hallucinatory realm hinted at in fits and flashes. These heads are somber and awesome, not without a sense of tragedy, but with a larger sense of life beyond it.

INK STICKS AND A SCROLL

The time came when even the gouache medium was hard for Park to handle. Lydia Park looked around the art stores to see if there was anything he could use. She hit on ink sticks — the tubes of alcohol ink with felt nibs — and bought all eight available colors. She bought typewriter paper; from a supermarket she bought a roll of shelving paper thirteen inches wide, thirty feet long.

Park began using the ink sticks with enthusiasm. He had used one of the earlier felt-nib alcohol pens back in the late forties soon after they appeared on the market; at that time the only color available was black.

At first, Park used the colored ink sticks on single sheets of paper. He drew figures in interiors, men against houses, faces.[71]

A little later he started on the roll of shelf paper. The texture of this is almost like a thick Japanese rice paper; it is woolier, more porous and felt-like than typewriter paper. The ink sticks still created a sharp edge when he wanted it, but they also blended together easily and could be spread out into broad areas of tone. He developed a technique of drawing in a few initial outlines in pale yellow, which would disappear underneath the heavier colors he laid on top.

It had not been Lydia Park's intention that the roll of paper be used as a continuous scroll; she had thought he would want individual pieces cut off. By the time he had completed his first scene or so, however, Park obviously was thinking of it as a scroll. The entire thirty feet are a continuous flow of one scene into another. It is like a marvelous, spontaneous jazz improvisation. There are a few passages where the transition from one idea to another is abrupt, but for the most part one idea develops out of another with exhilarating sureness and inventiveness.

The Scroll (nos. 74a-d), which has no title beyond that, could be said to have a "subject." It is like a Sunday afternoon walk on a spring day along sidewalks and through a great public park like the Boston Common he knew as a boy. It is Park's "Park" and he may have been aware of this play on words. The scroll recalls not what was specific and particular but what was general and enduring about the small public pleasures he knew in his youth.

It is a work of remembrance in other ways: a great many subjects are familiar ones Park had used before. Some of them had not appeared in his work for twenty-five years; some are from the early and middle thirties, some from the early fifties. As in the last oils and gouaches, Park developed not one subject alone but played on the whole repertoire of subjects and motifs he had used over the years.*

The first scene shows a view of a street. To the right is a public building with a flag flying. To the left is a porch of some sort; a young man leans on the porch post.[72] In the foreground, a very large head of a woman stares at the viewer. The scene abruptly changes to a yard. There is a flowering tree, then a fence leading up to a house. The extreme perspective in the representation of the fence is a distinctive early new figurative device which appeared in many paintings of the early fifties. A woman opens a door of the house and a dog runs out to the street where another woman wearing a hat and veil pulls on conspicuous black gloves while talking to a young man. The dog and the woman with hat and gloves recall the satiric caricature figures of the early fifties. After this brief appearance, nothing in this particular tone of early caricature appears again.

Instead, in the next picture, the predominant subject of the scroll, people in a park, is introduced. It is summer; the grass and the trees are yellow, a woman is in a bathing suit. In the background is an equestrian statue. Beyond, figures in shirtsleeves and light clothes sit around on park benches.

Suddenly, an enormous rear view of a voluptuous statue is thrust into the foreground. The play of large foreground figures against smaller ones in the background is typically Park. The motif of sculpture also dates from earlier. In the early thirties, he had been a stonecutter for the sculptor Ralph Stackpole, who was doing two giant figures for the front of the San Francisco stock exchange. In those days, he did many paintings of sculptors at work — for example in the mural for John Muir School (DP1104). The statues in the scroll park provide him with an excuse to introduce the nude figure, but they are not only excuses for the nude. They are truly "statues," not just "nudes" and Park takes a certain sport in presenting them in a humorous light. Unlike the rest of the scroll which is brilliantly colored in the primary ink stick colors, the statues are done mainly in black and white in a manner recalling his drawings. The statues occur several times throughout the first half of the scroll.

Moving along the scroll, just beyond the statue — perhaps admiring her rotundity — are three sailors. They are logical inhabitants of a park, though there is no indication that Park himself had ever painted this subject before. The sailors are the vanguard of a crowd of figures moving into view from the right.

* *Note: October 1988* — The scroll is the subject of a remarkable act of publishing. Bedford Arts of San Francisco published *The David Park Scroll* in its entirety in the accordian-fold manner the Japanese developed to reproduce oriental scrolls. The book was suggested by the author, who wrote an afterword for it. It is the only opportunity to see the scroll in its original colors, using the author's color slides taken in 1961-62 when the ink stick colors were fresh and unfaded. Through the intervening years, the colors have faded, despite precautions the University of California at Berkeley took to protect the scroll with sliding shutters except when being viewed.

For a moment, almost the whole lower half of the picture is filled with heads. The crowd subject had interested him off and on throughout his new figurative work. There are crowds on beaches in the early fifties, crowds on campus in the later years. Here in the scroll, the heads in the crowd resemble certain single late heads in oil; the features of the faces are enormous in relation to the heads.

Above the crowd stretch several long, horizontal branches of trees. These occur a number of times in the painting and help to give it more of a sweep and a horizontal continuity.

Just beyond the crowd, which appears to be walking along the shore of a little river, the picture opens up into a wide vista. A graceful pedestrian bridge arches across the stream to another shore. In the distance, a tower, reminiscent of Boston's Bunker Hill monument, rises into the bird-filled blue sky. Everywhere, people loiter or pursue summer pleasures. The bridge itself is another of those diagonal perspective lines, shooting with abrupt foreshortening into the distance. A sculptured cupid at one end of the bridge balustrade carries on the statue motif.

On the stream beyond the bridge are two rowboats, each with two figures. In a work of reminiscence, figures in a rowboat have a special nostalgia: not only had the rowboat subject interested Park in his last decade, it was the subject of the earliest known drawings from his childhood *(no. 33)*. Here, boats skim across the glittering reflections on the surface, oars extended, looking like waterbugs, brilliant in reds, blues and yellows. Further downstream, past a little beach with sunbathers on the near shore, the scroll reveals a floating boat dock and a cluster of rowboats waiting for hire.

Just beyond, looking down over the stream at the boats and a swimming swan, is a mother and child. The mother holds her hand upward, supporting the little child, who sits on her shoulder. Here again a subject from the past re-emerges; the mother-and-child subject had been one of his favorites in the middle thirties, when his own children were young. It did not reappear for over a decade, but during this final period he returned to it several times.

The next subject on the scroll is a less familiar one. It is a crowd of young people coming from a building, perhaps students coming from a school. The building itself is a neoclassic structure which has been developed by Park with unusual attention to detail in the columns of the portico, and the sculptured lions by the entrance. In the yard of the school is a little fountain or birdbath, supported by a cluster of cupids; two birds flutter down to the water. Two women with a look of the school teacher about them stride militantly across the yard.

The scroll moves on to a sculptured pool. In the center of the fountain is a nude statue of a woman. Her pose is contorted in such a way that even though she is large, her entire figure is contained within the confines of the scroll. She obviously caused Park a certain amount of trouble, as well such a complicated pose might; he drew and redrew her in pale yellow lines before applying the heavier dark lines over. Behind her is another row of statues, only partially within the picture; their exaggerated poses mimic neoclassic sculpture and probe its vulnerabilities in a typical Park fashion.

At the farther edge of the round pool stand a boy with a balloon and a girl holding a ball; they watch a group of boys playing ball on the lawn. The birdbath, the pool, the balloon — round motifs begin to occur with increasing frequency.

Beyond this group is a great crowd on a hillside above a baseball diamond, where a game is in progress. It is Park's only known baseball picture, though he did a football painting in the mid thirties. The intense yellow and white light on the diamond almost suggests artificial light, though the scroll otherwise is clearly in daylight. Just beyond, the crowd at the baseball game curves around and pushes to the foreground of the scroll again. Above the crowd is an awning with great yellow and red stripes, recalling the awnings which appeared in many of the street scene paintings of the early fifties and in a few of the paintings of the thirties. Foremost in his crowd is another enormous head, this one of a young woman.

The scene changes. For a moment the viewer is looking through two large windows into the interior of a restaurant or club. Men dressed in formal-looking black are seated around red tables; there is a coffee cup and perhaps a glass. Figures around tables are a familiar Park theme, but the formality of the scene is puzzling. Beyond these figures in the rear of the scene are more windows, through which a palm tree is visible. The scene looks somehow like an unusually staid and formal sort of jockey club at a racetrack. Beyond this puzzling moment more familiar Park subjects return. The scene is outdoors again; it is a yard with flowers and trees. In the distance, people in informal clothes are sitting around tables, reminiscent of the patio of the mid fifties. In the foreground is a heavy-set man wheeling a wheelbarrow. He wears an armless undershirt unlike the T-shirted figures of the fifties. He is straight out of the W.P.A. mural days; he recalls the workers, one of whom pushes a wheelbarrow, in the John Muir School mural. Hardly anything comparable to him had occurred in Park's art for twenty-five years.

Beyond this scene, a walkway along the edge of the park emerges, with lawns and daffodils on one side, apartment houses on the other. Among the figures on the walk is a little boy running, pulling a helium-filled balloon along by a string. The round balloons and the horizontally curving strings are continued further along the walkway in a group of boys and a mother with a child in a baby buggy in front of typically Boston apartment houses.

Beyond the boys with the balloons, at last we come upon a balloon seller, an old Italian man with a great swarm of balloons all straining at their strings, moving upward out of the picture. It would seem as though he has been moving through the park ahead of us, selling a balloon here and there; we come upon them with increasing frequency, and at last we come to the source. A little boy reaches upward, wanting one of the balloons; his mother stands behind him.

The old balloon seller is an enigmatic figure. He is clearly a type, though Park never painted types; he is an old Italian man with curly grizzled hair and a mustache, with a broad, round black hat with a red rim; there is something almost melancholy about him. Who is the balloon seller? Perhaps he has no special meaning, but somehow it seems as though he does.

Beyond the balloon seller is the final episode. The round circles of the balloons change to more ominous circles. It is a street scene, not unlike the scene at the beginning of the scroll, with a school or some other sort of public building at the end. There is a truck, with round tires; there are street lamps with round lanterns. Then there is a round white clock on the school building, and a round black clock on a pole on the shadowy side of the street; both say it is four o'clock. In the center of this last street is a large round sign on a pole; it says "DEAD END." In its center is a tiny black skull and crossbones. The round circle of the sign stands out aggressively against dark black and purple lines, somehow hesitant and uncertain, which lie beyond it on the darkly shadowed side of the street. Later, when Park signed many of these last ink stick works in fountain pen, he signed the scroll with his name in the middle of this sign.

The scroll as a whole is a gay one; it is a happy dream of childhood. The Dead End sign comes as a shock; it is the first — and only — overt indication of Park's awareness of death, though it was, in fact, created when he knew only that he was ill, not after he knew he was dying. According to Lydia Park, the scroll was painted with lightness, with mockery and wit. Park could seldom resist debunking anything serious or pretentious; perhaps he could not escape feeling this way even about the possibility of his own death. It is entirely consistent with his personality that he should have such an attitude.

His brother, Richard, also says he saw the completed scroll as early as January or February 1960, several months before cancer was diagnosed. The Dead End subject was prompted, as he says, more by a metaphysical, prophetic sense of his impending end than by any medical knowledge.[73]

Beyond that, however, there is something in the end of the scroll, in the crescendo of roundnesses, the balloons, the clocks, the sign, something in the old balloon seller himself, which hints at a private and unrevealed symbolism.

A remarkable and unique work of art, the scroll was presented to the University of California at Berkeley in memory of Park by Mrs. Benjamin Lehman, and was installed in the Student Union center, Zellerbach Hall.

This scroll was not the last of such efforts for Park. He wanted to do others. He was not able to handle anything that ambitious again, but he did do several sequences three or four feet long and about half the width. There is a rollicking couple of trapeze artists, swinging horizontally along the page (DP112). There is a string quartet *(no. 32)*, a remarkable reinterpretation of the same motif which had interested him so much in the early thirties. There is something on the order of a Roman bath sequence (DP110), with nudes like his late oils, though with more decorative details.

A shorter sequence (DP109) presents two large heads, one profile, one full-face, both in the act of lifting African-like masks to their faces. There is much of the theater about these heads and masks. Oddly, this is a subject which Park had almost never used before, even though it was in every way a natural one.* Even as a child, Park had liked puppet theaters. In almost all his teaching positions, he had been involved with school theatricals and scenery. He had also designed the sets and costumes for a Darius Milhaud opera. Lydia Park was reminded of a Eugene O'Neill play they saw in which the parts were represented by life-size puppets. The

---

* See footnote on page 27 about Park's Federal Arts Project mural for Mills College, which included, amongst its toga-clad figures holding musical instruments, one woman holding a giant mask, referring to the dramatic arts and evoking the large theater masks of ancient Greece. The mask of Park's last works did, indeed, have a precedent.

appearance of this new mask motif during these last few works is an indication that Park was still developing new ideas as well as reminiscing over old ones.

DEATH

David Park died September 20, 1960, at his home in Berkeley. George Staempfli, his New York dealer, wrote the author a statement which describes these last days.

> *"In September 1960, I flew out again to San Francisco to see him once more if it was possible. I knew that he was very ill at that time and that he didn't have long to live. I called up Deed [Lydia Park], and she said he did want to see me and to come out the next afternoon. Apparently, they shot him full of morphine before I arrived, and when I came, he was able to talk a little. We spent perhaps half an hour going together through his last batch of watercolors and gouaches. He was only a ghost of his former self except for his eyes which were sharp and penetrating. At one point I said I liked one gouache particularly because of the weight of the figures sitting in it, and David looked at me and said with a try for a smile, 'You're telling me.' Somehow the whole experience of all his years of painting was right there in those words. He had known what he had been doing all along, and had simply gone on doing it.*
>
> *He died early the next morning, and the day after, Deed, Elmer Bischoff, Dick Diebenkorn and I went through all the pictures in the house to try and list them and date them. It was a strange afternoon, in a way, almost a gay one because so much remembered pleasure and fun came into it. Deed was wonderful and held on to herself magnificently. When I left that evening, I felt that I had witnessed some of the best stuff human beings are made of, and I was proud to know these people and to have been with them."*

A number of memorial shows were held. The Staempfli Gallery presented an exhibition of the work of Park, Diebenkorn and Bischoff in November 1960. The Oakland Art Museum presented an exhibition of drawings, gouaches and ink stick drawings in December 1960, which was also shown at the Art Center in La Jolla in February 1961 and the Cooperative Gallery in Sacramento in March-April 1961. A major retrospective exhibition was initiated by the Staempfli Gallery in December 1961 and toured the country for a year. It was shown at the Institute of Contemporary Art in Boston, the Tennessee Fine Arts Center at Cheekwood in Nashville, the Corcoran Gallery of Art in Washington, D.C., the Oakland Art Museum, the University of Minnesota Gallery in Minneapolis and the Krannert Art Museum, University of Illinois, in Urbana. An exhibition of Park's work during his university years was held at the University of California Berkeley campus art gallery in fall 1964 and circulated to other campus galleries.

70. Others are: *Head* (DP548), *Double Portrait* (DP535), *Head* (DP54), *Head with Red Collar (no. 70).*

71. DP96, DP97 and many in DP552-687 list.

72. This is much the same Boston world as *City Street (no. 28).*

73. Letter from Richard Park to the author, July 25, 1964.

Part Five

THE QUESTION — WHAT PLACE IN AMERICAN ART?

O ne of the principal questions in a discussion of David Park and new figurative painting during the fifties was whether or not there really was something which could be called a new figurative movement, a new post-abstract direction in American painting, and whether there was a distinguishable California expression of it. The principal artists themselves, the writers on art, and the broadening world of younger artists and students became entangled in some way with this question.

THE ARTISTS' VIEWPOINT

The California artists most involved — Park, Bischoff and Diebenkorn — never attempted to launch a movement. They did, in fact, much to discourage such an idea.
        Park spoke very consistently about new figurative painting being only a variation of abstract expressionism. In 1952, he had written,

> *"I believe the best painting America has produced is in the current non-objective direction. However, I often miss the sting that I believe a more descriptive reference to some fixed subject can make. Quite often, even the very fine non-objective canvases seem to me to be so visually beautiful that I find them insufficiently troublesome, not personal enough."*[74]

In 1953, he made a distinction between his previous work as "paintings" and his new figurative work as "pictures," but he said,

> *"All of them are representations of definite subjects and otherwise probably not so very different from my former work."*[75]

In later years, he wrote occasionally about his work, but seldom explained its relation to abstract expressionism. In 1959 he told a reporter from *Time*,

> *"Before, I felt like a critic while I was painting, not a painter. Besides, I like bodies."*[76]

The three artists' reaction to the idea of a movement could be seen in their attitude toward the contemporary bay area figurative painting show organized by the author in 1957. The author talked a number of times to all three artists about the idea of an exhibition conceived as a debut of the movement. The name "New Realism" was presented and rather insisted on. After ruminating about all this for several weeks, Park gradually made their position clear. He said they did not want their work promoted as a new movement. They objected, not because they felt there was no justification for it, but because they disliked the whole business of "movements" in art. Park himself suggested the title "Contemporary Bay Area Figurative Painting." He felt it was a descriptive title for an exhibition, and would not be interpreted as the name of a movement. To him, "figurative" was an artist's word, clarifying what was meant without added associations.

THE CRITICS ANSWER

The national art press showed no reluctance to grapple with questions about new directions and movements. It took several years for California new figurative painting to get out of the regional columns and into widely-read feature articles in the national art magazines, but after that, discussion of the implications of this new "movement" or "school" were increasingly frequent. Most of this criticism was more hostile and suspicious than otherwise. Writers were quick to take exception to what they heard about these California paintings before they ever saw them. Though the attitude of many of the reviews remained critical, there was a steady retreat, a gradual acceptance of the individual painters, then of the group as a whole.

REACTIONS TO THE FIRST NEW YORK EXHIBITIONS

The early coverage of new figurative painting in the national art press involved not California artists but New York artists. Only later was it extended to the Californians. To understand the reactions to California artists it is necessary to consider what kind of reaction the New Yorkers got.

The first two new figurative artists to show in New York were Larry Rivers and Willem de Kooning. Larry Rivers had a show with a new figurative cast to it in spring 1949, but, since he did not have an established reputation as an abstract expressionist, it did not arouse a general feeling in the art press of a significant change in direction. There was a marked reaction, however, when de Kooning, one of the leaders of abstract expressionism, began exhibiting paintings with a figurative aspect.

During the mid forties de Kooning had done several of his series of *Women.* He destroyed most of them without exhibiting them, but one of the survivors was shown at the Janis Gallery in October and November 1950, in an exhibition selected by Leo Castelli, *Younger Painters — U.S. and France.* Young French and American artists of similar style were presented as pairs; de Kooning was paired with Dubuffet.[77] The reaction did not come, though, until his 1953 one-man exhibition at Janis. Sidney Geist wrote about it first. He said de Kooning

> *". . . has gone to the end of the expressionist line, and beyond. He has gone too far, but that is the only place to go."*[78]

A couple of weeks later a howl of anguish went up from Hubert Crehan. Calling de Kooning's new figurative concerns retrogressive, he stated for the first time the "failure of nerve" explanation which was given frequently by those who felt there could be no authentic defection from abstract expressionism.

In an article titled "Woman Trouble," Crehan wrote,

> *"de Kooning has feelings and ideas about the* Woman, *but he has not fused them. He has been traumatized by the subject; a fatal mistake for an artist, art and psychology being mutually exclusive. Striving after an apocalyptic vision of the* Woman, *he has produced for us a Medusa and for himself a dilemma. I believe this dilemma results from his tactic of returning to the subject after his earlier divorce from it. He can't paint without the* Woman, *yet he can't connect with her. . . This attempted reconciliation raises a question: has de Kooning given himself a decent chance to handle the idea of* Woman *by re-introducing the subject? The* Woman *is too awfully present. Does de Kooning, or any painter today, especially an artist who has previously jettisoned so many of the banalities of the associative encumbrances of the subject, does such an artist need an image to express an emotion in his work, even an emotion about* Woman? *Are we on the scene of a reaction? Is our revolution in painting imperiled so soon? . . .*
>
> *Art must be a wonder of poise and newness of feeling that takes us beyond outselves. But de Kooning, instead of striking forward to connect with his theme, has reeled and turned back to look for the* Woman.
>
> *Great creative expression in the arts is always an exploration into the unknown, and the artist in the vanguard, way out in front, can get lonely or hysterical; the inclemencies of the experience may drive him back to snug and familiar surroundings.*
>
> *de Kooning was out there in the unknown not so long ago, connecting with something new, something wonderful; but now he's back home again, reworking the image — and he hasn't connected."*[79]

Art criticism for some years was preoccupied with Crehan's question of whether or not the new figurative movement was a retrogression, caused by a lack of courage to continue the abstract expressionist direction. Most of the writers were avowedly sympathetic to abstract expressionism, and they often raised this question in such a way as to suggest it was a reactionary trend.

CALIFORNIANS IN THE NATIONAL ART PRESS

The California new figurative painters were slow to achieve recognition in the national art press. For the first seven years, mentions were confined to the regional columns from San Francisco and Los Angeles, and there were no shows, either one-man or group shows, of new figurative painting outside California.

There was, however, coverage in the regional columns from a very early date. *Kids on Bikes (no. 24),* the first widely known new figurative painting, was reproduced in *Arts Digest* in 1951,[80] accompanying a rather superficial review of a San Francisco annual, and there was no mention of Park.

The first written mention of California new figurative activities in the regional columns came in reviews of the 1953 San Francisco Art Association annual. Lawrence Ferling wrote about evidences of "objective expressionism" versus "abstract expressionism." He mentioned,

> *". . . painters in the show who have gone through abstract periods and are now producing objective-expressionist work. David Park's* Riverbank *and Elmer Bischoff's* Lake *are deeply subjective expressions, with color and form that succeed in creating the sensations of abstract painting."*[81]

In *Art News,* Erle Loran noted,

> *"Painting around San Francisco continues to look advanced, although the free form Abstract Expressionism so boldly developed through the influence of Clyfford Still and Mark Rothko has subsided to some degree. . . . A revolt within the original group was started by David Park in the form of painting realist subjects in an Expressionist manner. Elmer Bischoff has now followed his lead in a big, bold landscape, conventional in concept but Expressionist in execution."*[82]

Park's new figurative painting was described in an article by Alfred Frankenstein, art critic for the *San Francisco Chronicle,* in *Art in America*'s first issue devoted to "Americans with a Future," in winter 1954. Writing for "Northern California," Frankenstein chose three artists, one of them Park, whom he quoted at length, and depicted as

> *". . . one of a small group of artists in this area who have gone through the non-objective and returned to painting subjects drawn from nature."*[83]

Park, Bischoff and Diebenkorn all had shows at the Paul Kantor Gallery in Los Angeles during the mid fifties, Park in June and July 1954. Park's exhibition contained many of his satiric caricatures; reviewer Jules Langsner, quite probably encouraged by Kantor, saw Park as like the German Expressionists. He called Park

> *". . . a forthright expressionist with a predilection for heavy impastos. . . There is a grim note to many of these pictures, a mordant quality which Park accents by harsh color in thick swatches. This ferocious contemplation of human foibles is crystallized perhaps most clearly in* Cocktail Party, *a venomous commentary that might have been painted in the Berlin of the twenties."*[84]

Henry J. Seldis, in his column for *Art Digest,* put something like Crehan's question to the Californians for the first time in reviewing Bischoff's show at the Kantor Gallery early in 1955. He said the show

> *". . . leads to speculations about some sort of 'return to nature' evidenced by an increasing number of younger abstract-expressionists. . . does this phase represent a reaction or does it reflect a search for a synthesis between image and abstraction?"*[85]

Another mention in a San Francisco column came from Herschel B. Chipp in 1956, writing about the exhibition of West Coast painting selected by Grace L. McCann Morley for the Sao Paolo biennial, which included Park's *City Street (no. 27).*

> *"David Park's personal, independently developed realism is daring — like the Romantic artist running on the rooftops — and narrowly avoids the chasm of the window-on-the-world concept of perspective. His sharp awareness of object-image relations strains to span the gap between the canvas and the world, assisted materially by sensuous paint webs."*[86]

The California new figurative painters first broke out of the regional columns in the national art magazines with a lavishly illustrated article by Chipp on "Diebenkorn Paints a Picture" in May 1957.[87] Chipp wrote sympathetically about the unusual metamorphoses of Diebenkorn's images, about his concern with the inter-relationships of figure, environment and abstract form. Since he was writing for a series of articles on how painters paint, Chipp naturally emphasized process. He chose not to become involved with Diebenkorn's relations to other figurative painters, in California or elsewhere; he neither asked nor answered questions about new directions and retrogression.

The politics of style came out in another major article the same year. "Figurative Painters in California," describing the Oakland Art Museum exhibition, appeared in *Arts* in December 1957. It reflected the magazine's partisanship for abstract expressionism, and stated the standard question about new figurative painting in particularly flamboyant terms.

> *"Audiences in other areas of the country — and above all in New York — may have some difficulty in distinguishing the specifically "California' elements in this new work, or indeed, in distinguishing it from similar efforts which they may have noted among artists in their own home ground. The audience for this new painting will also want to determine whether... it represents a new pictorial strength, or, as its adversaries have argued, it is merely a new failure of nerve in the face of the challenge which the so-called 'heroic' period of American abstract painting laid before a younger generation."*[88]

The 1957 Oakland show was also given an extensive review in Herschel B. Chipp's "San Francisco" column in *Art News.* He analyzed the three principal artists at some length, finding Park's figures and compositions "Impressionist" in character, but stating that,

> *"The reality of these paintings resides not so much in the figures themselves as in the movements of a heavily charged brush that has built up thick, sensuous layers of blended pigment...."*

Chipp noted that Park became increasingly involved with heavy paint,

> *"... thus moving toward the absorption of the figurative aspects into the reality of the surface."*

Chipp also restated the now classic question about figurative painting, but more objectively and with more concern for the subtleties which underlie the question. He said,

"The controversy stimulated by this exhibition is both heated and prolonged. One spokesman for the Clyfford Still tradition brands the movement as retrogressive and an 'easy way out.' On the other side some make predictions of a new realism that will render abstract painting démodé, and they herald its appearance as 'The Next Direction.' But the most important question to ask is not whether any of the artists represent or do not represent the human figure or any other 'thing,' but whether in making a painting where the artist represents the forms of things, he makes the realness of these things invoke a corresponding realness in the pictorial presence of the picture. This problem of assimilating the shapes of the things of the real world into the picture bears the constant hazard that the pictorial realities of the painting may be inhibited or disrupted. Both these directions are seen here."[89]

It can be seen from these articles that statements were obviously given different meanings on different coasts. The new figurative artists in California, and even California writers, never made assertions on behalf of a general new stylistic movement. These faint stirrings out in California were seen by the more belligerent partisans of abstract expressionism in New York to be a battle flag, and some were quite outspoken in their self-defense against a new figurative style or any other Californianism. After the first California new figurative paintings were seen in New York in 1958, and after one-man shows for Diebenkorn, Park, Bischoff, James Weeks and others, the paintings came to be judged more on their actual merits.

In fall 1959, George Staempfli presented a David Park exhibition to inaugurate his new gallery. The show received some of the most favorable criticism of any of the new figurative shows in New York. "A.V." in *Arts* acknowledged Park as the "grand-daddy" of the bay area figurative painters, and said,

"Park has created a figure that has many effects of reality. . . but whose ultimate reality is overridden. . . and that may be why even their evident heartiness, their solidity and strong color can be taken as a lament, and why this most rigorous of 'abstract configuration' presents, finally, the strongest statement of some cruel contemporary paradox. This general concern. . . he has made most intensely his concern, and most successfully."[90]

"I.H.S." in *Art News* said,

"In his concern with sensuous paint matter and with immediacy, Park is related to current Action Painting. He does not discover his image in the process of painting but uses the painting to describe the image. However, both are so fused that Park manages to avoid using Action Painting as decoration."[91]

Dore Ashton, writing for *Arts and Architecture,* was the only strong voice of dissent. She found the paintings inexpressive and repetitious.

"The David Park exhibition at the new Staempfli Gallery was a great disappointment. It had been heralded as 'The Real Thing,' the germinal source for the whole West Coast figurative movement and I was naturally

hopeful that it would provide a raison d'être for the recrudescence of
figure painting. It did not."[92]

The first New York group show of California new figurative painting was the
Park, Bischoff, Diebenkorn show, held as a memorial to Park, in November 1960
at the Staempfli Gallery. The *Arts* reviewer, "M.S.," still started off with a quick
assertion that ". . . their approaches are too divergent to constitute a school," but it
is, on the whole, a favorable review, especially for Park, who

> ". . . stands out as the strongest and most mature, in that his works are
> fully realized; though he was unknown in the East until last year, his
> reputation will now surely soar."[93]

"I.H.S." in *Art News* attempts to find something of the West in these
paintings.

> "His sun-drenched bathers at one with nature might be twentieth-century
> counterparts of the pioneers who trekked west."[94]

A major retrospective show, organized by the Staempfli Gallery and
presented in New York in November 1961, with six subsequent showings in
museums throughout the country, brought the most serious critical consideration of
Park. In the popular press, the show received a feature review from *Time,* which
said,

> "Dying of cancer at 49, he never fulfilled his own promise as an artist; yet
> his achievement was sufficient to make him one of the most significant
> U.S. painters of the 1950s."[95]

In the art press, the exhibition was reviewed in a feature article by Sidney
Tillim.[96]
Sidney Tillim is of special interest; he was the first reviewer on a magazine
which had been a stronghold of abstract expressionism to take new figurative
painting or other "new realisms" seriously. In place of the earlier point of view,
wondering whether such painting represented "a failure of nerve in the heroic age
of American abstraction," Tillim saw it as a style of great potential significance;
this is true in spite of endless fault-finding and qualifications along the way.
He wrote in April 1961,

> "From exhibition to exhibition, the tremors in the crust of modern style are
> growing in intensity. Representational art is the mountain thrusting
> through the plain. For my part, it is the painting I am now most interested
> in. I find that it gives me more to look at and more to 'understand.'
> I appreciate its ring of familiarity and I believe it has a future."

But he felt that new representational art did not yet have a secure place: it was not
yet "a complete art form," it had not "disproved the allegation that it is old hat."[97]
He felt the interest in California painters was really encouraged by commercial
dealers, who needed something "new" to follow up on the successes of the New
York school. He wrote careful reviews of Diebenkorn's[98] and James Weeks' shows,
in the course of which he gave his definition of the movement:

*"... his [Weeks'] paintings are demonstrably San Francisco in style,
featuring the heavy, fluid pigmentation, the broad approach to figuration,
and, in general, the almost piously heroic attitude toward its 'new'
realism which results in very sizable canvases."*[99]

He hardly granted it existence before he wondered if it had not become a
formula. He felt the common style of all the artists involved overshadowed the
individual distinctions; that they were already so predictable they even shared the
same faults.

In Tillim's review of the Park retrospective, he describes Park's career as
a partial victory over American provincialism. He discusses the question of a new
figurative art only briefly.

*"Park's repudiation of Abstract Expressionism anticipated if it did not
inspire what is today the San Francisco School... whose public success
effectively dramatizes the failing powers of Abstract Expressionism..."*[100]

He states that, in his later new figurative work, paint itself, used in an abstract
expressionist manner, becomes the true subject, while Park simultaneously revives
the provincial, neo-classical ideals of the art of his childhood, represented by the
nude, as the ostensible subject. He concluded,

*"... the more violent his work became, the more elegiac was its persistent
nostalgia for an art of some magnificence that would not seem to be
superior to its environment."*[101]

EXHIBITIONS

Certain national exhibitions of figurative painting have affected the atmosphere in
which the new California paintings are seen nearly as much as the articles in art
magazines. Two exhibitions with special relevance were the *New Images of Man*
exhibition at the Museum of Modern Art in 1959 and the University of Illinois
exhibition in 1961.[102]

The tone of the Museum of Modern Art show was totally different from that
of new figurative painting in California, as Peter Selz, who organized the exhibition,
saw the new art pushing into even more difficult discords than abstract
expressionism.

Selz found this new work to be a spasm of terrorized protest against the
horrors of the modern world.

*"These images do not indicate the 'return to the human figure' or the 'new
humanism' which the advocates of the academies have longed for...
There is surely no sentimental revival and no cheap self-aggrandizement
in these effigies of the disquiet man.*

*These images are often frightening in their anguish. They are created
by artists who are no longer satisfied with 'significant form' or even the
boldest act of artistic expression. They are perhaps aware of the
mechanized barbarism of a time which, notwithstanding Buchenwald*

and Hiroshima, is engaged in the preparation of even greater violence in which the globe is to be the target. . . . 'Only the cry of anguish can bring us to life.'"[103]

It was unquestionably the most important exhibition of new figurative work held to date in this country; Selz's catalogue alone was a major effort. The exhibition seemed to claim that this new art is more difficult, more bitter, than what had gone before and must, therefore, be more vital and significant. In contrast, the California painters, especially Park, made a conscious effort to avoid being involved in the increasing emphasis on discord. The tone of Park's work is optimistic, based on an interest in the pleasures of life.

The second exhibition was the University of Illinois exhibition of *Contemporary American Painting and Sculpture for 1961.* It took a "return to figurative subject matter" as its theme. Each artist was asked to comment. Bischoff's and Diebenkorn's replies expressed an indifference if not a contempt for movements, and asserted the importance of the individual. The younger painters were more willing to meet the question on its own terms; many answered in the affirmative.

If one were to decide whether or not a widespread new figurative direction existed in American painting on the evidence of these statements, one could only conclude that most mature artists distrust and resist the existence of movements of any sort in painting, but that a great many artists, including the young new figurative painters in California, definitely sensed the emergence of a new interest in figurative art. James Weeks and Nathan Oliveira had major New York shows. William Brown, Joseph Brooks, Walter Snelgrove and others achieved national recognition. A number of painters who came to this style later, like Joan Brown and James Jarvaise, had important shows. It is also true that some prominent young painters like William Wiley returned to abstract expressionism after a period of new figurative painting.

A group of new figurative styles developed in spite of any attempts to ignore them or to explain them out of existence. David Park was the first in California to turn from abstract expressionism to a new figurative style, and among the first few in the country to make such a change. The paintings of Park, Bischoff and Diebenkorn and of other bay area painters constitute a related, distinguishable new figurative direction.

Park's new work not only raised questions and partisan feelings about its relation to abstraction. His work also raised the broader question of New York's relation to the rest of the country.

The implication of much that had been written and done in New York is that, since it had become a capital of modern art, any significant new direction in American art would normally stem from there. When new and distinctive work, especially new movements, occurred outside the city, something should account for the fact. The most common explanation is the "regional" one, according to which the art in question rose to significance by exploiting some localized, regional quality which distinguishes it from the more generalized, cosmopolitan art of New York.

Park was the first artist in California to challenge so much of this image New York had created for itself. He developed his new figurative manner early and independently, and he neither sought nor acknowledged a regional quality.[104]

Most New York art press reactions inseparably tangled the question of regionalism with the question of figurative and abstract styles. Some tended to dismiss Park and the rest as having no "California" qualities already known in New York, and therefore as merely provincial.[105] Others strained to find regionalisms and to defend them on that basis.[106] The position that these artists were of the same order of significance as creative artists in New York, without any predominant regional characteristics, was difficult for the critics to entertain,[107] and was only accepted slowly.

The fact that Park's work presented a regional as well as a stylistic challenge accounts, in the author's opinion, for some of the early reluctance by Eastern cities to acknowledge any significant accomplishment by him. One challenge could not be accepted without the other. The charge of retrogression so often levelled at Park and the rest revealed not only the stylistic challenge but also inherently raised the regional challenge as well. The many critics who felt some uncertainty about one or the other easily adopted both concerns.

However independent of New York Park was in the formation of his new figurative manner, it should be acknowledged that it became primarily a New York context in which he and the others have been seen. The response from the galleries and publications in New York came largely because the question of a move from abstraction to figuration had already been raised within New York circles. The fact that Park and the others have all disliked emphasis on style, movements and regionalisms, preferring stress on the individual artist's accomplishment, has to some extent been lost in the midst of more typically New York concerns. And these painters and the art circles in California accepted readily enough the recognition and success which came from New York, however New York chose to look at and describe their art. In whatever manner it was put, this recognition was the first acknowledgment by New York that a creative act of the highest order of significance to contemporary painting could now occur in California.

74. *Contemporary American Painting*, 1952, University of Illinois, Urbana, Illinois, 1953, p. 220.

75. *The Artist's View*, September 1953, no. 6.

76. *Time*, November 9, 1959, vol LXXXIV, no. 19, p. 83.

77. See Belle Krasne, "Youth: France vs. U.S.," *American Digest*, November 1, 1950, vol. 25, no. 3, p. 17. See also: Thomas B. Hess: "de Kooning Paints a Picture," *Art News*, March, 1953, vol. 52, no. 1, p. 25; "E.K.", *Art News*, April 1949, vol. 48, no. 2, p. 46; Harriet Janis and Rudi Blesch, *de Kooning*, N.Y., 1960, p. 58.

78. Sidney Geist, "Work in Progress," *Arts Digest*, April 1, 1953, vol. 27, no. 13, p. 15.

79. Hubert Crehan, "Woman Trouble," *Arts Digest*, April 15, 1953, vol. 27, no. 14, p. 5. Crehan is using "connection" in reference to the motto of E.M. Forster's *Howard's End*, "Only Connect." See also: James Fitzsimmons, "Art," *Art and Architecture*, May, 1953, vol. 70, no. 5, pp. 4-8; Elaine de Kooning, "Subject: What, How or Who?", *Art News*, April 1955, vol. 54, no. 2, p. 61.
     In January 1956, Hubert Crehan did battle with the image of a "California School" or an "Ecole du Pacifique" of abstract expressionism which had been publicized in New York and by Michel Tapie abroad. (Hubert Crehan, "Is There a California School?", *Art News*, January 1956, vol. 54, no. 9, p. 32.) Crehan insisted that no such school existed, though he was reverential about the days of Still and Rothko at the California School of Fine Arts when Crehan himself had been a student there.

The way the article is written would make it appear that Crehan was totally ignorant of the new figurative work of Park, Bischoff and Diebenkorn.

80. *Arts Digest,* March 15, 1951, vol. 25, no. 12, p. 10.

81. "San Francisco," *Arts Digest,* February 15, 1953, vol. 27, no. 12, p. 10.

82. Erle Loran, "Art News from San Francisco," *Art News,* March, 1953, vol. 52, no. 1, p. 41.

83. Alfred Frankenstein, "Northern California," *Art in America,* Winter 1954, vol. 42, no. 1, pp. 48, 49.

84. Jules Langsner, "Summer in Los Angeles," *Art News,* June 1954, vol. 52, no. 4, p. 58.

85. Henry J. Seldis, *Arts Digest,* February 15, 1955, vol. 29, no. 4, p. 15.

86. Herschel B. Chipp, "Art News from San Francisco," *Art News,* September 1956, vol. 55, no. 5, p. 18.

87. Herschel B. Chipp, "Diebenkorn Paints a Picture," *Art News,* May 1957, vol. 56, no. 3, pp. 44-47.

88. "Figurative Painters in California," *Arts,* December 1957, vol. 32, no. 3, pp. 26, 27.

89. Herschel B. Chipp, "Art News from San Francisco," *Art News,* December 1957, vol. 56, no. 8, p. 50.

90. "A.V.," "In the Galleries," *Arts,* September 1959, vol. 33, no. 10, p. 60.

91. "I.H.S.," "Reviews and Previews: New Names This Month," *Art News,* September 1959, vol. 58, no. 6, p. 12.

92. Dore Ashton, "Art," *Arts and Architecture,* December 1959, vol. 76, no. 12, pp. 7, 8.

93. "M.S.," *Arts,* November 1960, vol. 34.

94. "I.H.S.," *Art News,* December 1960, vol. 59, no. 8, p. 15; Eleanor C. Munro, "Figures to the Fore," *Horizon,* July 1960, vol. II, no. 6, pp. 16-24.

95. *Time,* April 27, 1962, vol. LXXIX, no. 17, pp. 48, 49.

96. Sidney Tillim, "Month in Review," *Arts,* March 1962, vol. 36, no. 6, pp. 36-40.

97. *Ibid.*

98. Sidney Tillim, "Month in Review," *Arts,* April 1961, vol. 35, no. 7, pp. 46-49.

99. Sidney Tillim, "Month in Review," *Arts,* January 1961, vol. 35, no. 4, p. 46.

100. *Op. cit.*

101. *Ibid.,* p. 37.

102. Indiana University's "New Imagery in American Painting" of 1959, in which Park's *Double Portrait* (DP535) was included; Contemporary American Realistic Painting," shown at the Albany (New York) Institute of History and Art, Crandall Library, Glen Falls, New York, and Skidmore College, Saratoga Springs, New York, in 1959 and 1960, in which Park's *Bathers* (DP514) was included. Other exhibitions of new figurative painting which indicated the growing interest in it were: "The Figure in Contemporary American Painting" circulated by the American Federation of Arts in 1961, which included Park's *Boy in Striped Shirt (no. 10);* "The Emerging Figure" at the Contemporary Arts Museum in Houston in May and June 1961; a special exhibition at the Institute of Contemporary Art in Boston; and an exhibition circulated by the Museum of Modern Art in 1962.

103. Peter Selz, *New Images of Man,* Museum of Modern Art, New York, 1959, p. 12.

104. Eleanor C. Munro, "Figures to the Fore," *Horizon,* July 1960, vol. II, no. 6, p. 114.

105. Anonymous editorial comment, "Figurative Painters in California," *Arts,* December 1957, vol. 32, no. 3, pp. 26, 27.

106. *Op. cit.,* which contains an elaborate literary comparison of California and its relation to New York with the Campana and its relation to ancient Rome.

107. See Sidney Tillim's reviews, cited above.

BIBLIOGRAPHY

*A*mong the principal objectives of this book were to work directly from paintings and drawings of Park and to assemble information on him directly from those who knew him well. The principal sources of information have been notes taken during a series of interviews with people close to Park. Perhaps twenty discussions were held with Mrs. Park, now Mrs. Roy Moore; she did much to make this book as honest and accurate as it is. She also assisted the author in examining and photographing paintings, in assembling drawings, scrapbooks and memorabilia, and in establishing contacts with certain people. Interviews were held with the following artists and friends — Elmer Bischoff; Bertrand Bronson; Richard Diebenkorn (three interviews) and Phyllis Diebenkorn; James McCray; Glenn Wessels; Hassel Smith; Mark and Ruth Schorer; Mrs. John F. Truesdell (Park's aunt); Tom Holland (a student of Park's); and Fred Martin.

In addition, the author obtained a lengthy statement from George Staempfli regarding Park, and had other letters or comments, including one from his brother, Richard.

Published material was also used fully to the extent that it existed up to 1962. A few references are included which are later than 1962. For comprehensive references from 1962 to the present, see the bibliography of the catalogue for the David Park exhibition presented by the Whitney Museum of American Art, November 1988-January 1989.

BOOKS

Hunter, Sam, *Modern American Paintings and Sculpture,* New York, 1959.

Barr, Alfred H., Jr., *Picasso: Fifty Years of His Art,* New York, 1946.

Janis, Harriet and Blesh, Rudi, *de Kooning,* New York, 1960.

Selz, Peter, *New Images of Man,* The Museum of Modern Art, New York, 1959.

MAJOR EXHIBITION CATALOGUES

(Only those catalogues which have some major statement by or about Park are listed below. Other catalogue references are listed in the footnotes.)

Contemporary Bay Area Figurative Painting, illustrated, with text by Paul Mills, Oakland Art Museum, Oakland, California, 1957.

Contemporary American Painting, University of Illinois, Urbana, Illinois, 1952, with statement by Park, p. 220.

David Park — Recent Paintings, illustrated, with foreword by Thomas Carr Howe, Staempfli Gallery, New York, 1959.

David Park — Exhibition of Paintings, with statement by Park, M.H. de Young Memorial Museum, San Francisco, California, 1959.

Contemporary American Painting and Sculpture, University of Illinois, Urbana, Illinois, 1961, pp. 150-151.

MAJOR ARTICLES IN PERIODICALS

Crehan, Hubert, "Is There a California School?", *Art News,* January 1956, vol. 54, no. 9, pp. 32-35 plus.

The Artist's View, David Park Issue, September 1953, San Francisco, California, no. 6.

Monroe, Eleanor C., "Figures to the Fore,"*Horizon,* July 1960, vol. II, no. 6, pp. 16-24 plus.

Arts, "Figurative Painters in California," December 1957, vol. 32, no. 3, pp. 26, 27.

Crehan, Hubert, "Woman Trouble," *Arts Digest,* April 15, 1953, vol. 27, no. 14, p. 5.

Chipp, Herschel B., "Diebenkorn Paints a Picture," *Art News,* May 1957, vol. 56, no. 3, pp. 44-47.

Tillim, Sidney, "Month in Review," *Arts,* March 1962, vol. 36, no. 6, pp. 36-40.

A FEW PUBLICATIONS SINCE 1962

Albright, Thomas, *Art in the San Francisco Bay Area 1945-1980,* University of California Press, Berkeley and Los Angeles, 1985.

Armstrong, Richard, *David Park,* exhibition catalogue, The Whitney Museum of American Art, New York City, 1988.

Berkson, Bill, "David Park: Facing Eden," *Art in America,* October 1987, (no. 10), pp. 164-171, 199.

David Park (1911-1960), exhibition catalogue, with writings by Howard Baker, Carl Belz, Richard Diebenkorn, Henry Geldzahler, David Park and Phyllis Tuchman; Salander-O'Reilly Galleries, Inc., New York, 1987.

McChesney, Mary Fuller, *A Period of Exploration: San Francisco 1945-1950,* The Oakland Museum Art Department, 1973.

Mills, Paul (Afterword), *The David Park Scroll,* Bedford Arts, San Francisco, 1988.

Measurements are in inches;
height precedes width —
o/c denotes oil on canvas.

LIST OF ILLUSTRATIONS

*T*his list is basically the list in the 1962 manuscript. Then, very nearly all the works belonged to Lydia Park, who gave permission for their reproduction and photography, these photographs being the ones used here. It seems in the best interest of all to provide as current information on ownership as possible. Though it is inevitably less than totally current, the effort has been made.

Some dates Park himself signed on his paintings. Many of them are informed speculation by Lydia, the author, and others. The "DP Catalogue" given to the Oakland Museum, but not able to be located at present, indicated which was based on a date signed by Park, and which was speculation. Without that catalogue at hand it is impossible to indicate which is which. Further, the speculation by various of us at various times produced slightly different dates. The Art Department, the Oakland Museum registration records indicate a great many of the paintings in the Mrs. Roy Moore gift of 1985 are datable to 1953. I think a certain number could well be, but doubt that so many are. I have therefore not quoted this 1953 date from the museum records.

This updating has been achieved with the very generous assistance of the Whitney Museum of American Art, Salander-O'Reilly Galleries, Maxwell Galleries and Staempfli Gallery. Undoubtedly, some works will have changed hands again since. There are also many cases where the present owner is unknown. In these cases, the 1962 owner is still listed (i.e. "1962: Lydia Park, Berkeley, CA").

If you have more current information to enter in the record, send it to the following, to record in their library reference copies of this book — everyone involved will be grateful:

Library, Whitney Museum of American Art, 945 Madison Avenue, New York, NY 10021; Library, Art Department, The Oakland Museum, 1000 Oak Street, Oakland, CA 94607-4892; Paul Mills, care of Capra Press, P.O. Box 2068, Santa Barbara, CA 93120.)

NOTES ON A CATALOGUE

Information on individual paintings and drawings from all sources was organized into a catalogue in 1961-62. Most were still owned by Lydia Park. There are over 700 catalogued works. Information includes size, medium, owner, inscriptions, labels, dating information, where reproduced and exhibited if known, pertinent comments, and photographs if available. The original is deposited with the Art Department of the Oakland Museum. (At the time of this publication, the catalogue could not be found; since it is a unique copy, it is very much to be hoped it comes to the surface soon.) Numbers in parentheses in the text, for example *Manicure* (DP15), refer to this catalogue. The numbers were determined by ownership at the time of cataloguing in 1961-2 — one through 400, Lydia Park, Berkeley; 500 through 999, consigned to Staempfli Gallery; 1000 through 1499, private collections, with the Richard Park group at Staempfli being the 1200s; paintings known only through reproductions, 1500s.

Most of Park's paintings in the bay area in 1961 were examined. In addition, an extensive collection of photographs has been assembled. This includes approximately 350 color photographs, almost all of which were taken by the author with the exception of a group of paintings in Richard Park's home in Washington, D.C., and others in the Staempfli Gallery supplied by the gallery, totalling about 50 from other sources. The photographs are in the Oakland Museum.

Figure, 1959, o/c, 20 x 16, (DP66). 1962: Staempfli Gallery. *(no. 68)*

Four Men, 1958, o/c, 57 x 92, (DP504). Whitney Museum of American Art, New York, NY. Purchase with funds from an anonymous donor, 1959. *(no. 67)*

Head, 1959, o/c, 19 x 16, (DP65). Mr. and Mrs. Jimmy Younger, Houston, Tx. *(no. 69)*

Head, 1960, gouache on paper, 11¹/₂-13? x 9¹/₂ (sight), (DP104). Nancy Park, San Francisco. *(no. 72)*

Head with Red Collar, 1959, o/c, 19 x 16, (DP79). Mr. and Mrs. Roy Moore. (Called *Boy with Red Collar* in the 1988 Whitney Museum exhibition catalogue.) *(no. 70)*

Interior, 1957, o/c, 54 x 48, (DP2). Mr. and Mrs. Carl Lobell, New York, NY. *(no. 63)*

Jazz Band, 1954, o/c, 24 x 36, (DP34). Fred and Natalie (Park) Schutz, San Jose, Ca. *(no. 30)*

Kids on Bikes, 1950-51?, o/c, 48¹/₄ x 52, (DP550). The Regis Corporation, Minneapolis, Minn. *(no. 24)*

Mother and Child, 1938-39?, o/c, 32 x 26, (DP1217). 1962: Richard Park Group, Staempfli Gallery. *(no. 14)*

Newspaper, undated, o/c, 14 x 18. Art Department, The Oakland Museum; gift of Mrs. Roy Moore, 1985. *(no. 9, color)*

Non-Objective (also called *Still Life — Non-Objective,* which is clearly self-contradictory; the author should have clarified this long ago while there was a chance of getting pertinent information about it), 1949, o/c, 34 x 25, (DP43). Art Department, The Oakland Museum; purchased by the Women's Board of the Oakland Museum, 1962. *(no. 4, color & no. 21)*

Nude, 1958, o/c, 28 x 14, (DP48). Mr. and Mrs. Roy Moore. *(no. 59)*

Nude Green, 1957, o/c, 69 x 56, (DP501). Hirshhorn Museum and Sculpture Garden, Smithsonian Institution, Wash D.C. *(no. 61)*

Nude (Unfinished), 1959, o/c, 29 x 36, (DP32). 1962: Lydia Park. *(no. 65)*

Portrait of David Park by Richard Diebenkorn, 1955, pencil on paper. Mr. and Mrs. Richard Diebenkorn. *(no. B, on page 2-3)*

Portrait of David Park by Richard Diebenkorn, undated, pencil on paper. Mr. and Mrs. Richard Diebenkorn. *(no. D, page 31)*

Portrait of David Park by Richard Diebenkorn, undated, ink on paper. Mr. and Mrs. Richard Diebenkorn. *(no. E, page 122-123)*

Portrait of Elmer Bischoff, 1955, o/c, 34 x 25, (DP42). Lydia Park. *(no. 44)*

Portrait of E. Bischoff, 1957, o/c, 22 x 20, (DP74). Corcoran Gallery of Art, Wash D.C. *(no. 45)*

Portrait of Hassel Smith, 1951, o/c, 33³/₄ x 28, (DP33). Mr. and Mrs. Wilfred P. Cohen, New York, NY. *(no. 23)*

Portrait of Lydia Park, o/c, (DP70). 1962: Lydia Park. *(no. 79)*

Portrait of R. Diebenkorn, 1957, o/c, 20 x 18, (DP75). Corcoran Gallery of Art, Wash D.C. *(no. 43)*

Profile and Lamp (Lydia Park), 1952, o/c, 16 x 13³/₄, (DP56). Mr. and Mrs. Martin Bookstein, Roslyn Harbor, NY. *(no. 76)*

Quartet, 1960, ink sticks on paper, 9 x 15¹/₄, (DP111). Mr. and Mrs. Roy Moore. *(no. 32)*

Rehearsal, 1949-50?, o/c, 46 x 35³/₄, (DP23). Art Department, The Oakland Museum; gift of an anonymous donor through the American Federation of Arts, 1962. *(no. 5, color & no. 22)*

Rowboat, 1958, o/c, 57 x 61, (DP512). Museum of Fine Arts, Boston, Mass. *(no. 78)*

Riverbank, 1956?, o/c, (DP509). Williams College Museum of Art, Williamstown, Mass. *(no. 80)*

Self Portrait, undated, pencil on paper, 8 x 7. Art Department, The Oakland Museum; gift of the estate of Marian Simpson, 1979. *(no. C, page 4)*

Shore Line, 1952, o/c, 32 x 38, (DP37). 1962: Lydia Park. *(no. 38)*

Small Head, 1958, o/c, 11 x 9, (DP106). Mr. John Bergruen, San Francisco, Ca. *(no. 83)*

Solitaire, 1954?, o/c, 30 x 24¹/₄, (DP50). Art Department, The Oakland Museum; purchased by the Art Guild of the Oakland Museum Association, 1962. *(no. 2, color & no. 40)*

Sophomore Society, 1952-53?, o/c, 38 x 46, (DP25). Corcoran Gallery, Wash D.C. *(no. 77)*

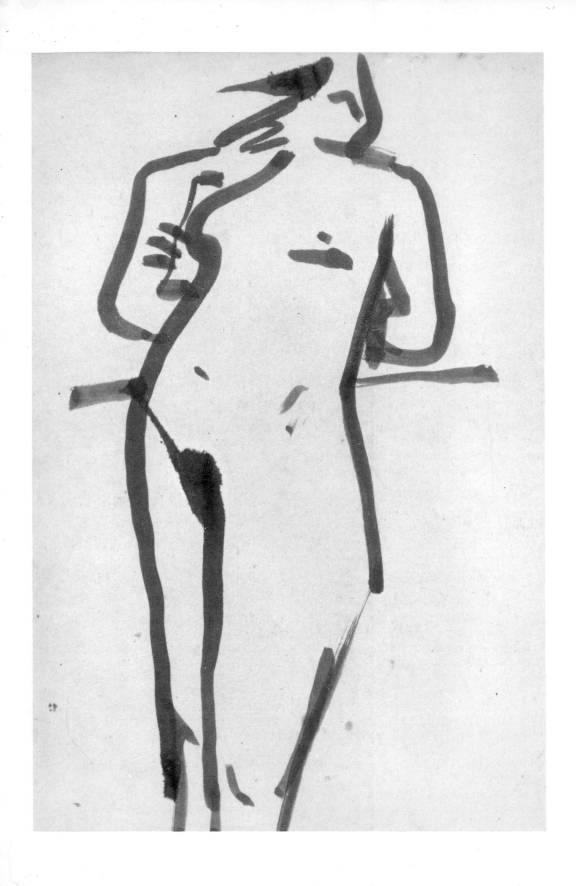